LANDSCAPES
OF THE WORLD

Created by olo.editions
www.oloeditions.com
15, rue d'Aboukir
75002 Paris
France

EDITORIAL
Nicolas Marçais
Claire Chamot

DESIGN
Philippe Marchand

LAYOUT
Manon Bucciarelli

TEXTS
Sophie Thoreau

TRANSLATION
Eleonore Morena

PROOFREADING
Maren Lange

COLOUR REPRODUCTION
PGY

Cover credits: (right) ©Cosmo Condina/Photolibrary.com;
(left) ©Imagemore Co, Ltd./Getty; ©Arctic-Images/Getty; ©Frans Lanting/Corbis.

Printed in Singapore by Tien Wah Press

ISBN : 978-2-9532483-1-9

LANDSCAPES OF THE WORLD

100 LANDSCAPES WHICH AMAZE, INSPIRE, INTRIGUE

INTRODUCTION

Our planet is under threat. At a time when environmentalists are sounding the alarm on risks linked to global warming, this collection of photographs aims to raise greater awareness, helping its readership discover, understand and last but not least act. The Earth has always given humankind everything it needs: food for sustenance, materials for shelter and the stuff of dreams. It also represents our origins as well as our future, teaching us life and humility. We are but very small in comparison and natural catastrophes remind us of this fact increasingly often. Man has succeeded in making the most of this world but must be careful not to deplete it. We must use our science with caution in order not to squander this heritage, leaving nothing for future generations. What would become of them tomorrow if this original paradise were to turn into a living hell? Where would we go? "Now more than ever, all the Earth's inhabitants must make solidarity their utmost priority" (Albert Jacquard). It is hard not to be touched by the Blue Planet's beauty and diversity. And all the more so when you really start getting to know it! It is home to so many fabulous landscapes, shaped over thousands of years by the ever-changing vagaries of the elements and their outbursts of fury: volcanoes gushing forth the newest of features, oceans shearing off the coasts, wind and rain sculpting the rocks, dormant fire under our feet, and ice cracking and splitting. Man has been venturing into space for a few decades now but is yet to elucidate the Earth's mysteries. There are still remote lands to be discovered and new secret worlds to be conquered and, more importantly, preserved. Open this book as you would a treasure chest; turn its pages and let those jewels trickle between your fingers; let your mind travel far out to sea and beyond the mountains to far-off countries with breathtaking scenery, fashioned by the hand of God. Get ready for the trip of a lifetime!

UNDER THE COBBLESTONES...
GIANTS' CAUSEWAY, IRELAND

Some 40,000 hexagonal cobbles make up this causeway, said to be created long ago by two feuding giants, one Irish, one Scottish.

All that remains of this rather spectacular paved road is the beginning and the end, in Northern Ireland, near Bushmills, County Antrim and on the island of Staffa in Scotland respectively. The Giant's Causeway forms a huge headland out to sea, made of juxtaposed lava prisms that fit perfectly together. Some only measure a few inches and the largest more than 30 feet high. Geological research carried out on this site provided more information on the volcanic activity that shook up the area during the Tertiary Period. Indeed, this irregular paving is the result of sudden cooling by the sea of an old basaltic lava flow dating back 50 million years. Out at sea lies the wreck of the Girona, one of the invincible Spanish Armada's galleons that sank straight to the bottom after smashing against the rocks during a storm. It has remained here on the seabed for four centuries, hiding its fabulous treasure.

IN LEAPS AND BOUNDS
PERITO MORENO, ARGENTINA

In southern Argentine Patagonia, the Perito Moreno runs down the Andes Cordillera like a river of ice, at a speed of 6.5 feet per day!

The star glacier of the Los Glaciares National Park is five times as big as Manhattan, boasts a two and a half mile front and rises 200 feet above the surface of the water. It was named after the expert (*perito* in Spanish) Francisco Moreno who worked on redefining the border between Argentina and Chile in the 19th century. This UNESCO World Heritage Site (since 1937) is one of the rare glaciers not threatened by global warming. It is fed by the 3rd largest fresh water reserve in the world. This wall of ice periodically forms a natural dam in one of the stretches of Lake Argentino, forcing the water to rise up to 82 feet before breaking under the pressure of the water in an unsettling crash that can be heard for miles around. Icebergs then start to drift into the Magellan Strait. Some are so thick with ice that they appear sapphire blue in color. The collapse of these jagged glacier blocks makes for a gripping sight and a few victims every year amongst those foolhardy enough to want to take a closer look at the giant's fall.

CHOCOLATE DROPS
CHOCOLATE HILLS, BOHOL, PHILIPPINES

Much like chocolate drops stretching away as far as the eye can see, these hills are one of the main natural attractions in the Philippines.

Legends abound regarding the Chocolate Hills and all include giants. Who else, in fact, could have succeeded in lining up 1,268 to 1,776 identical hills, 98 to 160 feet high, over more than 20 square miles? The most beautiful of these stories is undoubtedly that of the giant Arogo who fell in love with a young local beauty, Aloya. When she died, he did not stop crying for hundreds of years. His tears petrified into rows of eternal relics symbolizing his sorrow. These marine limestone hills, sculpted by the elements over the centuries, owe their name to the grass that covers them and turns chocolate brown in the dry season. Listed as a National Geological Monument, the Chocolate Hills have been proposed by the Philippine authorities for inclusion on the UNESCO World Heritage List.

SUNRAY PLEATS
ANTELOPE CANYON, ARIZONA,
UNITED STATES

Antelope Canyon changes costumes with the passing days and seasons much like fairy tales princesses with their sunny and starlit dresses.

In 1931, a simple Native American shepherdess, looking for one of her sheep, by chance discovered the most accessible part of these incredible Arizona gorges, also known as Corkscrew Canyon. This monument's story (the site is still owned by the Navajos) was written over the course of 150 million years ago. The wind and beating rain eroded the desert of sand, hollowing out narrow gorges over a stretch of five miles, sculpting the different layers of sandstone into fabulous striped and multicolor drapes. The highest part of the site – 4,000 feet above sea level – is also the easiest to reach and therefore attracts more visitors than the lower, steeper area. The sun shining through the light shafts makes the colors sing out in hues of ochre, crimson and violet and sets these walls ablaze at sundown… Terrific flooding in Antelope Canyon still occurs and can be fatal, as was the case in 1997. Lost sheep beware…

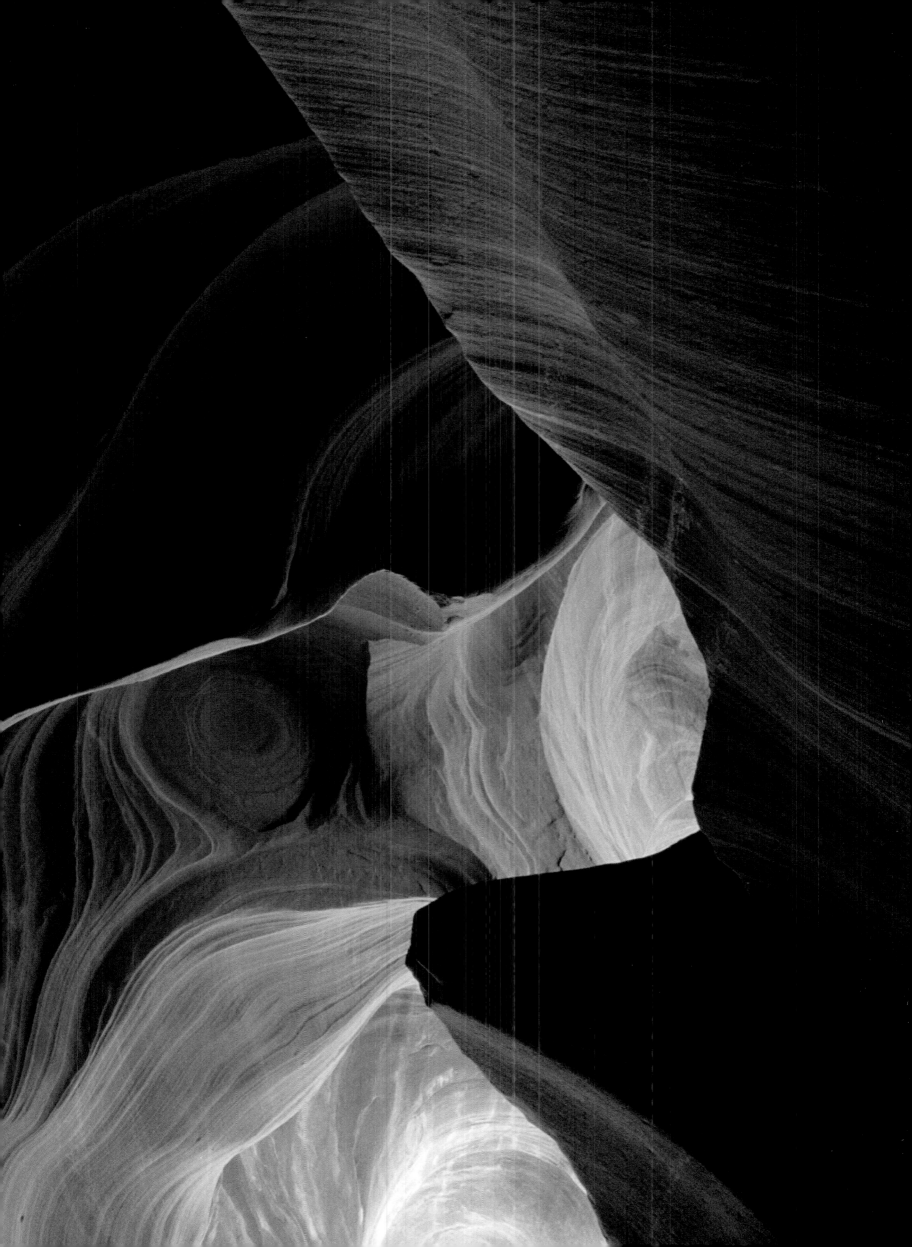

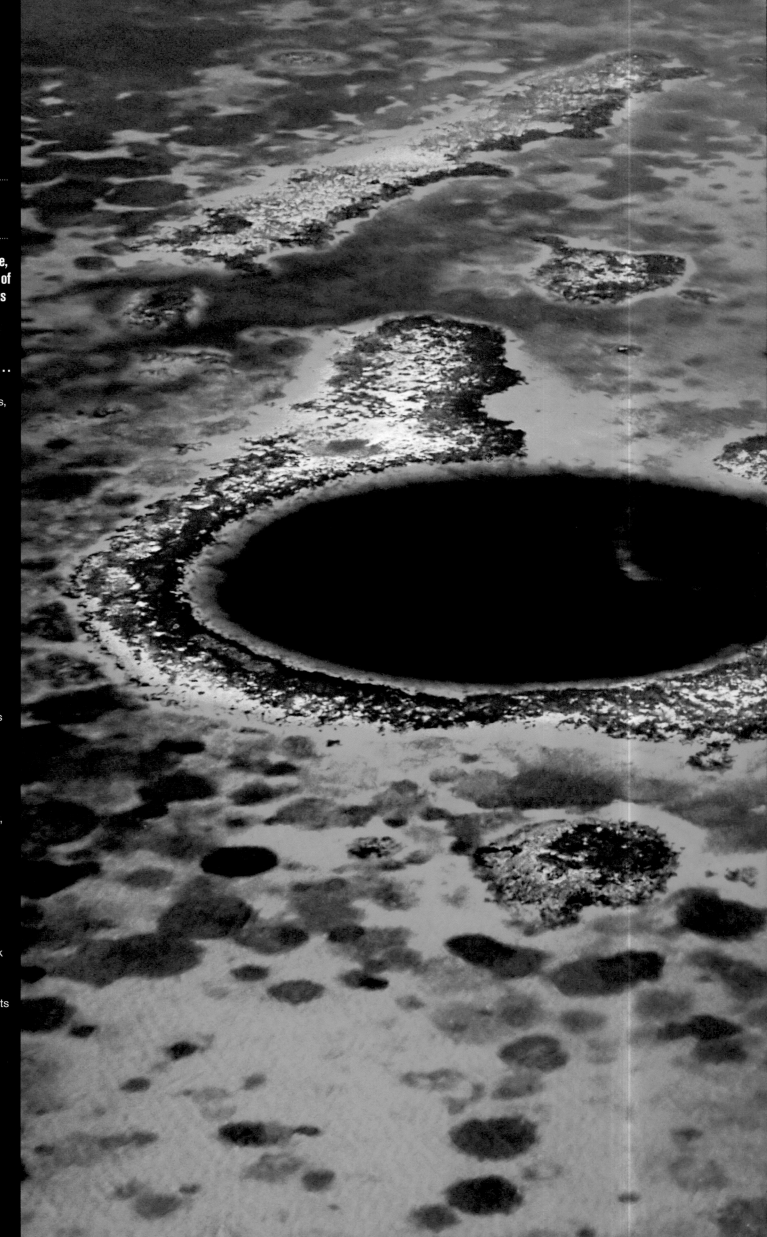

BLUE EYE
GREAT BLUE HOLE, BELIZE

This underwater sinkhole, 62 miles from the coast of Belize, was made famous by Jacques Cousteau. A legendary vertical abyss for divers as well as the superstitious among us…

It is said to be bottomless, haunted by a monster of the seas. The Mayas believed that these "mouths" allowed you to communicate with the other world. The reality is just as fascinating: this perfectly circular fault, 1,000 feet across and 400 feet deep, was formed as a terrestrial cave system, which was submerged at the end of the Ice Age and had its roof collapse in during earthquakes. Huge stalactites (some 26 feet high) and various tunnels that lead to caves where turtle bones were found remain as vestiges from this era. Jacques Cousteau brought back the first pictures in the 1970s and, from his boat, the *Calypso*, the man with the red sailor's cap charted the depths of this blue sinkhole, one of approximately 180 in the Caribbean. In these year-round 75°F waters, there is little life, due to the lack of direct sunlight. All that you come across are a few solitary sharks, tourists like us.

PINK ON RED
LAKE NATRON, TANZANIA

When Lake Natron drinks too much, it has no qualms about crossing the border with Kenya to spill its excess waters loaded with red algae, incidentally pink flamingoes' favorite food.

Lake Natron is what is known as an endorheic lake: it cannot flow into the sea and has no other choice than to widen its shores when drenched with water, as is the case here, under particularly tormented skies. Its surface area (370 to 810 square miles), depth (no more than 10 feet) and volume vary with the seasons. Located in a branch of Africa's Great Rift Valley and fed with rainwater from three neighboring volcanoes, it was once a fresh water lake before evaporating over time. In the dry season, when temperatures reach 122°F, this basin of slimy water with a pH close to that of ammonia is saturated in soda, salt and bacteria favorable to the proliferation of red algae (which give it its color), pink flamingoes' favorite food. Up to two and a half million of these colorful birds gather here during the mating and nesting season. The camouflage is guaranteed!

WHITE HELL
DEATH VALLEY, CALIFORNIA,
UNITED STATES

Deep within this arid valley, the ground scorches your feet at 194°F and the air burns your lungs at more than 133°F. There are even record highs in the shade, if you can find it…

Covering an area a little larger than the size of Connecticut, Death Valley is a record-breaking site. It is one of the largest deserts in the United States, has one of the highest peaks, the Panamint Mountains, at an elevation of 11,049 feet, and one of its lowest points, the Badwater Basin, lying 282 feet below sea level. Ten thousand years ago, a large lake covered the bottom of the valley and evaporated due to global warming, leaving behind a lake of stagnant water, and more importantly a crust of minerals, salts and dried mud covering over 200 square miles. The mountains prevent the moisture of the Pacific Ocean from reaching this area and the burning winds do the rest. Record temperatures of 14°F in January and 134°F in July were recorded here in 1913. Approximately 1,500 species of plant and animals have succeeded in adapting to this climate, taking advantage of the cool of the night, when temperatures drops to a mere 95°F.

The Rock Islands may be lesser known than the Maldives or Tahiti but they are nevertheless considered to be one of the best diving spots in the world.

Though the Republic of Palau enjoys one of the highest standards of living in the Pacific Ocean, this 26-island and some 300-islet archipelago's true treasure lies just beneath the surface of the blue lagoon waters: a beautiful underwater world still totally intact. The crystal-clear sea of the Philippines provides a habitat for soft corals and thousands of small multicolored fish. Sharks rub shoulders with turtles, Napoleon fish and "devilfish" or manta rays. The islands, whose submerged areas span a mere 180 square miles, the equivalent surface area of Washington DC, are covered in lush vegetation that makes them look like mushrooms floating on water. They also abound in waterfalls, well-preserved caves and jellyfish-laden lakes, not to mention white sandy beaches where one can forget about the crazy world out there... lying among the water lily flowers.

THE ORIGINS
OF THE WORLD
MOUNT RORAIMA, VENEZUELA

You would hardly be surprised to come across a dinosaur at the foot of this mountain from another age, a site that inspired Sir Arthur Conan Doyle's *Lost World*, and more recently Steven Spielberg's *Jurassic Park*.

Mount Roraima is one of the most ancient geological sites on the planet, dating back a couple of… billion years. This rocky colossus is nearly 9 miles long and reaches 9,219 feet at its highest peak. It seems to appear miraculously from an ocean of greenery and mist, on the border of Venezuela, Guyana and Brazil. The forty or so tabletop mountains (*tepuyes* in Native American) formed after the separation of the South American and African continents, each harbor a unique ecosystem, a sanctuary for mostly endemic plant and animal species. Roraima's vertical cliffs have always fascinated climbers and adventurers.

POCAHONTAS' RIVER
CHICKAHOMINY RIVER,
VIRGINIA, UNITED STATES

This river runs in Native American territory and made life difficult for its habitants, whether in the days of the first settlers or during the American Civil War.

It owes its name to the Native American tribe that lived on its shores when the first white men landed at the beginning of the 17th century. It was traveling upstream, in the hope of finding a passage to the Pacific Ocean, that Captain John Smith was captured by warriors and saved by the legendary Pocahontas. Like a wild thoroughbred, the river can be docile and tame in dry weather but turns into impassable wetlands nearly one mile wide after strong rains and the spring thaw. It was this river, in fact, that put an end to one of the Yankees' attempts to take Richmond during the Civil War in the middle of the 19th century. Today, the river is a vital source of drinking water for an entire region of Virginia and a leisure area for sailing and fishing. Before turning into an estuary, it winds in and out of the vast swamps of New Kent County over a distance of 37 miles.

DEEP GORGES
GRAND CANYON, ARIZONA,
UNITED STATES

When you look right down into the Colorado River, you are in fact travelling back 1.7 billion years in time! The Grand Canyon's rocks are some of the oldest on Earth.

It may be the oldest and certainly the most spectacular, but it cannot claim to be the deepest! The Grand Canyon tells the story of the North American continent through 4,300 feet of strata – 6,600 feet in places – hollowed out over time by the Colorado River. A total of 40 different types of rocks have been found over the 280 miles spanning these gorges between Lake Powell and Lake Mead. The region's arid climate has meant that various fossils and the remains of extinct animals have remained perfectly preserved. Some present-day species are, in turn, threatened by deforestation and tourism. President Theodore Roosevelt said of the Canyon: "Leave it as it is. The ages have been at work on it, and man can only mar it." He surely could never have imagined that one century later, a billionaire would finance a huge glass U-shaped footbridge, offering tourists the thrill of experiencing the great void under their feet…

CELESTIAL FIRE
LIGHTNING, KANSAS,
UNITED STATES

Lightning strikes one hundred times per second on Earth! And storms make for quite a light and sound show, particularly when they feature thunder and lightning.

Lightning is static electricity discharged during a storm, brought on by a significant difference of electrical charge between two points (sometimes up to 100 million volts). A flash of light then streaks the sky at a speed of 25,000 miles per second, and an explosion – a cracking or drum roll sound – due to the release of heat (approximately 5,430°F) resounds: this is thunder. Lightning is most often white. It can take on a yellowish hue in the presence of dust, a bluish tint if there is hail, and even turns red in the presence of rain. It generally measures 12 to 13 miles long, but a record lightning bolt measuring 118 miles, the equivalent distance from Miami to Key West in Florida, was observed in Texas. To know whether thunder is close by, divide the number of seconds between lighting and thunder by five to calculate the distance in miles. Even though high up areas and prominent objects are more vulnerable, no one is ever safe from being struck by lightning!

SEA SHEPHERDS
KORNATI ISLANDS, CROATIA

Are these feminine curves at the surface of the water or meteorites fallen into the Adriatic? Kornati stretches out its string of bare and uninhabited islands over 115 square miles.

A Croatian saying goes that there are as many islands as there are days in the year. The more precise (or perhaps less poetic) cartographers' version lists 147, for the most part uninhabited. Five belong to the National Park created in 1980. However, the archipelago is essentially made up of small islands and rocks, bare or covered in scrub, olive, pine and wild fig trees. There are no beaches along the crystal-clear waters; rock has instead given its name to the site (*Kornati* or "Crowned Islands"). These dots of land lying off the Dalmatian coast are in fact mountain peaks submerged in the Ice Age, more than 20,000 years ago. A network of low stone walls crisscrosses the mineral landscape and helps keep sheep fenced in. Shepherds are indeed the only temporary inhabitants of these islets. In the summer season, they leave their small, basic houses by the water's edge, which are rented out to travelers looking for a little solitude and a return to nature, each set to become the new Robinson Crusoe.

LAYER CAKE
VERMILION CLIFFS,
UTAH / ARIZONA,
UNITED STATES

Nature has donned her most beautiful palette of colors, creating these Neapolitan slices of sandstone, clay and limestone rocks that stretch out over nearly 80 square miles on the Colorado Plateau.

Along with the Coyote Buttes, the Wave is without a doubt the most famous of these spectacular formations, part of which is known as the Grand Staircase, a stack of sedimentary layers of rock at different stages of erosion. These hills reach 3,000 to 6,500 feet at their highest peak and are streaked in yellow, orange, red and pink, primarily due to the iron oxide and manganese present in the rock. The most ancient features are 2 billion years old and the youngest a mere 40 million. The canyons are so narrow in places that only a thin blue ribbon of sky can be seen above. The décor is not only mineral: hanging gardens of ferns and orchids grow here and there, mountain sheep and pronghorns know the best grazing spots and, in springtime, rain covers the desert with a huge carpet of flowers, like a final impressionistic flourish to a painting.

ON THE ROOF OF THE WORLD
HIMALAYA, NEPAL

Imagine mountains as far as the eye can see, over an area twice as big as the state of Colorado. You are in the heart of the Himalayas, the "abode of snow" in Sanskrit.

This mountain range stretches out over 1,491 miles, covering 231,600 square miles from Pakistan to Tibet. Here, clouds brush shoulder with the peaks, fourteen of which reach heights of more than 26,250 feet above sea level, not least Mount Everest, the highest peak in the world. All have been conquered during innumerable expeditions led by experienced mountaineers, some of whom perished in the attempt. If these gigantic mountains have had limited human migration, they also protected India from the Mongolian invasions of the fearsome Genghis Khan. The Himalaya range was formed 70 million years ago, following a collision between the Eurasian and Indian plates. The latter continues to move about five cm per year, adding a few millimeters to the peaks of the Tibetan Plateau. The 29,029 feet of today's Mount Everest may be a higher figure than when we were taught at school, but is certainly less than the elevation that will be found in the schoolbooks of tomorrow.

MINERAL WATER
SPOTTED LAKE, CANADA

What is sky blue with large yellow polka dots? A unique phenomenon on this planet: the Spotted Lake in Canada.

This 37-acre lake located in British Columbia has unrivaled mineral content, including magnesium, calcium and sodium sulfates, as well as silver and titanium. At the hottest period of the year, water evaporates leaving behind multicolored pools of crystallized minerals, in yellows, blues and greens. These treasures are of course highly coveted. Thus, during the First World War, tons of minerals were extracted every day and used to make ammunition. The mud and water's healing properties when treating wounds, sprains, aches and skin diseases nearly led to the creation of a thermal spa. Native American tribes from the Okanagan Valley succeeded in their campaign to protect their sacred lake and keep tourists at bay. The neighboring highway is now the only point from which one can observe the Spotted Lake's polka dots, which change color according to the weather.

WATER CURTAIN
NIAGARA FALLS, CANADA

One could not imagine a more beautiful border between two countries: the most famous waterfalls in the world separate Canada from the United States.

12 million visitors a year come to admire them from the edge, the bridge, the sky, or even from underneath, thanks to a tunnel dug under the Canadian side of the Falls. And let us not forget the daredevils who brave death to go over them! The Falls are not the tallest in the world but are fascinating due to their width and the thundering power that supplies hydroelectric plants on either side of the border. Formed 12,000 years ago when the glaciers melted, the falls have gradually receded seven miles from their original location. The power of the water that bolts down 167 feet – the equivalent of a 16-story building – gnaws away three feet of rock every year. Niagara Falls is in fact composed of not one but three waterfalls: the Horseshoe, the American and the Bridal Veil Falls. In the very harsh winters of 1911 and 1936, the last two froze up entirely. Startling!

FIRE ISLAND(S)

GALAPAGOS ISLANDS,
ECUADOR

Each of the Galapagos Islands is a volcano, the oldest nearly ten million years old. Scarcely older than the marine iguanas and giant turtles…

Time does not seem to have a hold on this archipelago located 600 miles from the Ecuadorian coast. It would hardly be surprising to come across a few pirates stocking up on water and meat, as they did in the 17th century, along with British and American whalers. The 13 islands (4 of which are inhabited today), 17 islets and 50 reefs are the visible parts of a large underwater volcanic mountain range. That number is probably set to change. Indeed, some volcanoes are being eroded, are shrinking and are seeing their mountain range increasingly widen; others will emerge from the Pacific waters, following eruptions and lava flows. The Galapagos Islands are located on the planet's hottest point, a fragile area in the oceanic crust, which explains the intense volcanic activity and almost annual eruptions. This does not seem to bother the incredible fauna that lives on these basalt rocks; man is the only threat to the marine iguana, which swum here millions of years ago.

AN ETERNAL GREEN CARPET

BEAUMONT, KANSAS, UNITED STATES

Right in the middle of the United States, the largest tallgrass prairie in the world remains much as it was in the days of the pioneers and the Wild West. Well nearly...

Cattle now live alongside the herds of buffalo in these sweeping fields of grasses that sometimes measure up to 7 feet high. Too rocky and hilly for intensive agriculture, the Flint Hills have always been used for raising livestock. In this part of Kansas, listed as an ecoregion by the WWF, controlled burns (prairie burning) in spring are still carried out to clear and fertilize this amazing grassland made up of hundreds of varieties of wild grasses and flowers. This is one of the rare places in the United States where agricultural practices perpetuate ancestral Native American traditions. Tourism also plays on nostalgia: a few steam engines still travel along the old railway lines and you can spend your holidays in a 19th century pioneer wagon, living the life of a cowboy!

THE CRAZY VERTICAL
EL CAPITAN, YOSEMITE PARK,
UNITED STATES

To reach the top of this 3,000-foot granite rock face, there are two options: you can either take the hiking trail or try your luck out on the great rock face that defies climbers from the world over.

The name El Capitan is enough to give any mountaineer the shivers. Their playground is a true granite cathedral, formed 100 million years ago when the Ice Age carved these sheer landscapes into Yosemite Valley at the heart of the Californian Sierra Nevada. Set between the southwest and southeast face of El Capitan, the rocky outcrop christened "the nose" remains a must for mountain climbers, even if there are now a dozen other demanding routes to climb. Some spend days hanging from the rock face, sleeping in hammocks suspended above the void. Their only aim: reaching the top to admire the giant sequoias and the 2,425 foot waterfalls, unleashed by the spring's melting snows. At nightfall, at the end of winter, the Horsetail Falls reflects the setting sun and transforms itself into an incandescent torrent. Water, ice and fire reunited…

SAND SPHINX
RUB AL-KHALI, OMAN

In this desert as big as Texas, the dunes look like giant fingers, or perhaps the claws of a sphinx, stationed on the old incense trade route.

The changing winds fashion these growing but static star-shaped dunes (up to 650 feet high). This is the largest sand desert in the world; two million years old and as big as Texas, it stretches out over four countries: Saudi Arabia, the United Arab Emirates, Yemen and Oman. In this area close to the Yemenite border, known as Rub al Khali ("Empty Territory"), the temperature can reach 131°F and years can go by without there falling a drop of rain. Although these landscapes seem devoid of any life, Bedouin tribes, animals and plants have adapted to the conditions, much like the Oryx, a kind of antelope that can survive for months on end simply licking off the morning dew. The desert is as calm as the dromedaries that traveled these dunes in long caravans, carrying precious incense, until the search for black gold.

FLOATING ISLANDS
ICEBERGS, ANTARCTICA

White, blue, and even multicolored, hiding its bulk under the icy waters of the Poles: drifting ice floe ahead!

Icebergs are small chunks of glacier which, once out at sea, start their long wandering journey. Before breaking up and melting into the salty water, they travel thousands of miles following eccentric courses, tossed about by the winds, waves and currents. They are made of fresh water that is sometimes 15,000 years old and can take on surprising shapes, such as these hard candy icebergs with colorful stripes. The purest have a bluish hue, with areas of red, orange and green being due to algae, and grayish or brown tones to remains of moraines or volcanic ash. These giant ice cubes are closely monitored and are in fact listed according to size and shape. Whatever their appearance, 90% of their volume is submerged. The largest iceberg ever detected was called B-15 and when it broke away from the Antarctic 10 years ago, it measured 4,250 square miles, that is to say more than twice the size of Delaware. It continues to drift along the coast of Antarctica.

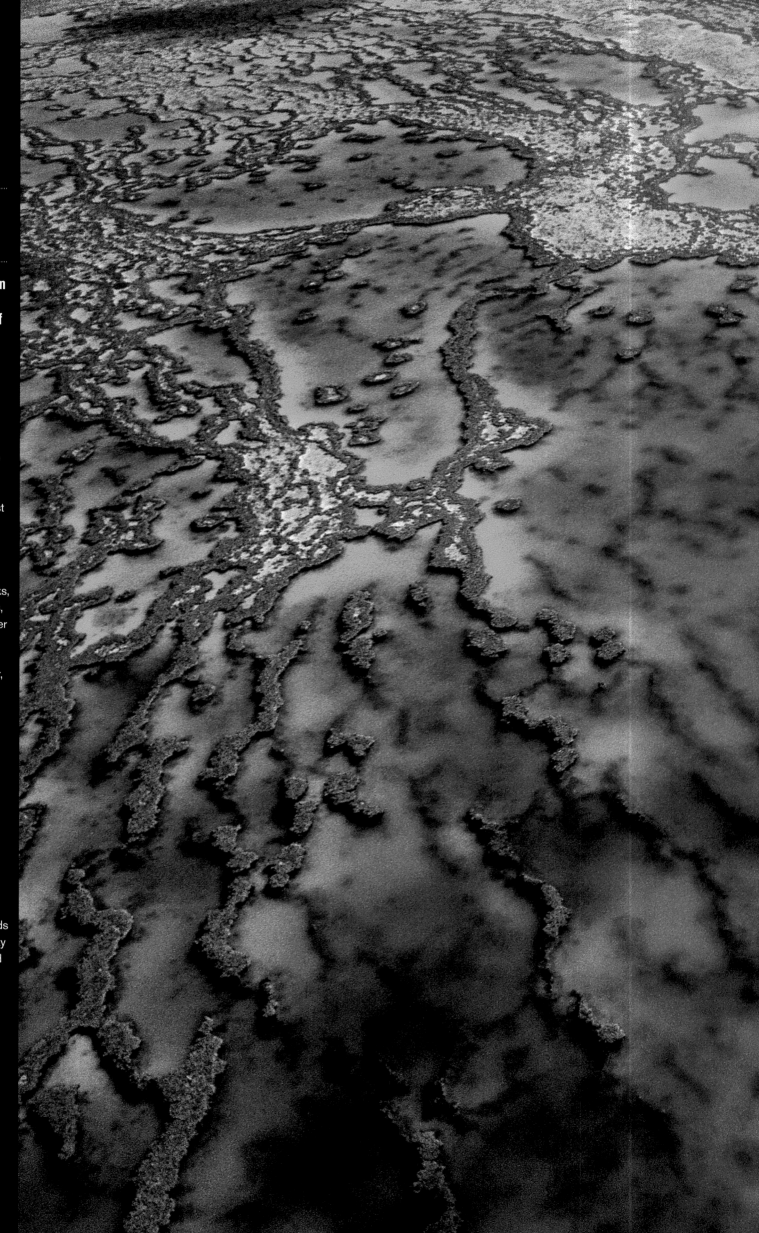

CORAL LACE
GREAT BARRIER REEF,
AUSTRALIA

This spectacle can even be seen from space: 133,000 square miles of coral reef, an aquatic paradise located along the eastern coast of Australia.

Seen from up high, the 2,000 islands and more than 3,000 reefs look like delicate lace floating on the turquoise waters of the Coral Sea. The largest coral reef in the world is home to 400 types of coral, more than 1,500 species of fish and 4,000 varieties of mollusks, not to mention anemones, sponges, worms and other crustaceans. Coral is not able to grow any lower than 100 feet underwater, making it a paradise for divers. It is, however, regularly damaged by cyclones and threatened by global warming, and a number of coral species are already living at their thermal tolerance limit and are starting to whiten and die. This strip stretches out over more than 1,250 miles from Bundaberg to Cape York and is also dotted with dream islands, white sands and tropical plants. Beauty surrounds you, above and below water.

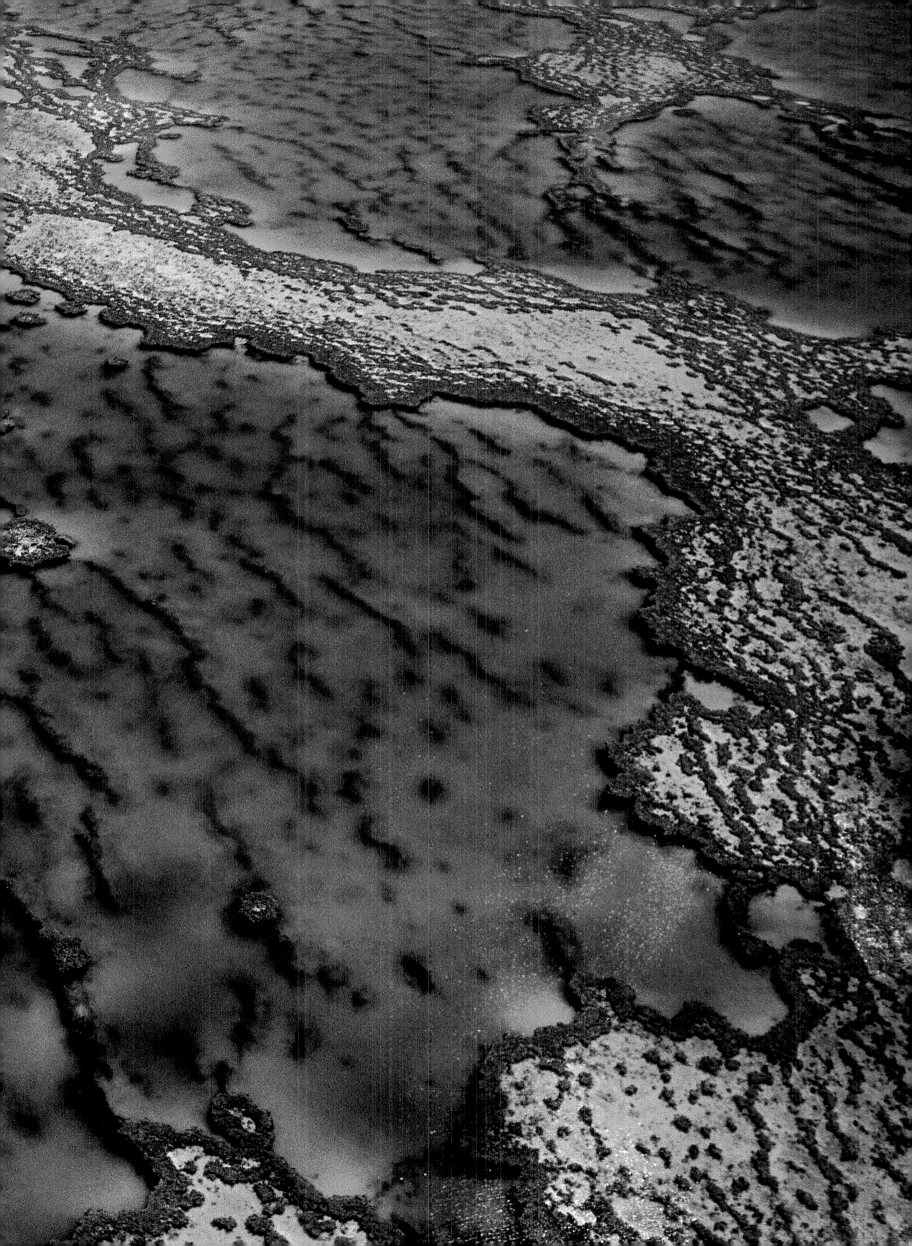

WILD HORSES
COLORADO RIVER,
UNITED STATES

Before being tamed by man, the Colorado River, wild and unbroken for millennia, ploughed its furrow through seven American states. A river of life...

It tears down the Rocky Mountains (13,927 feet), alternating rapids and calm waters, in order to flow into the Gulf of California, 1,450 miles downstream. For millions of years, this spirited river devoured river banks en route, snatching earth and rock from the Colorado Plateau to the point of hewing out amazing chasms, with 1,000-foot high cliffs, like the famous Horseshoe Bend in Arizona, and even 6,500-foot features in the Grand Canyon. The Rio Colorado (or "red river" in Spanish) owes its name to the silt and sediment carried by the waters. This ochre-colored earth has remained at the bottom of Lake Powell since dams were built. Now one of the most regulated and developed rivers in the United States, it brings water, and therefore life, to the states it crosses. This blue-green serpent in the middle of ragged landscapes is visible from space, 155 miles from the Earth.

DELTA RACEWAY
MACKENZIE DELTA, CANADA

What may look like a formula one racetrack from a bird's eye view is in fact a navigable channel of one of the world's biggest river deltas, covering an area the size of Connecticut.

The Mackenzie River has been carrying sand and silt along to the Beaufort Sea for thousands of years, gradually forming this 50-mile-wide delta, stretching across 5,200 square miles. The sweeping, fanned-out area is a maze of ever-shifting channels, shallow lakes and fleeting islands, in which water is more abundant than land. The only hills to be found in this flat country are conical mounds of earth covered ice called *pingos*. Arctic tundra covers the north whereas the south is a dense forest of spruce, poplars and willow trees, home to Canadian elks, beavers, foxes, and various species of fish. Inuit tribes have also inhabited this natural area since the dawn of time. Scientists use satellite technology to watch over this sweeping delta plain and to study the impact of climate change and the damage to the environment caused by the extraction of natural resources such as oil and gas.

MACHETE
FOREST, BORNEO

In Borneo, one of the last primary forests on the planet is being cleared and burnt. Biodiversity is being sacrificed on the altar of economic development.

On this island in the Indian Ocean, twice the size of Texas and less densely populated than the state of Kentucky, people still lived as they did in the Bronze Age up until the last century. That was before the arrival of multinational corporations. With backhoes humming, they cleared and burnt a quarter of the virgin forest in the space of ten years, aiming to secure a return to mining certain minerals, increase wood exports and develop oil palm cultivation. This giant fire, a huge source of greenhouse gases, was visible from space for months at a time! Aside from the primary forest, this primitive paradise is still very much undiscovered and home to various rare endemic species. The constant temperature of around 86°F, the 100% humidity, as well as the absence of light under the thick branches have created a unique world for carnivorous plants, flying lemurs, first-rate camouflage artists and tribes of... headhunters, recognizable by their lobster-shaped tattoos.

THE HANDS OF FATIMA
SAHARA, ALGERIA

The Sahara is the largest desert in the world, spans ten countries and is as big as the United States or China. The sun shines a record 3,723 hours a year.

In Arabic, Sahara means "Greatest Desert," and it lives up to its name: a desert of sand, stones and volcanic ranges like the Ahaggar, occupying a quarter of Algeria's total surface area. Erosion has sculpted grooves into these rocks, as well as sharp peaks such as the Assekrem Plateau at 8,950 feet above sea level, where Charles de Foucauld, an old French Colonial army officer, chose to set up his retreat more than a century ago. With its somewhat less extreme climate, the Ahaggar is an important place of shelter for hundreds of animal and plant species. It is also one of the territories of the "blue men", the Tuareg, nomad Berbers, descendants from the first North African inhabitants. In order to survive in these extreme surroundings, you have to learn about simplicity, much like the dromedary, capable of drinking 36 gallons of water in ten minutes then nothing for a month; or the small seeds that lodge themselves between the rocks and can resist drought for ten years, waiting for the next rainfall to come.

The Rio Kerep "swan dives" from the summit of Mount Ayuantepuy. These falls are one hundred times less renowned but twenty times taller than Niagara.

This is the world's highest waterfall, with a height of 3,212 feet, a plunge of 2,647 feet, and another more modest cascade at the bottom. It was discovered in 1933 by an American aviator, Jimmy Angel, who gave it his name. As he was flying over prospecting for gold, he spotted what looked like a sparkling fault in the vertical cliffs of one of Canaima's tabletop mountains. For a fleeting moment, he believed he had found the El Dorado, the River of Gold! A second expedition a few years later nearly took a nasty turn: his plane crashed into the summit of Auyantepui Mountain and it took him 11 days to get back to civilization. You have to work hard to see the Angel Falls as they are only accessible at the end of a fair walk through the jungle or after a long flight over Canaima National Park. This gateway to the Amazonian forest is also famous for its pink sand and gold and diamond mines where the Bolivar, a pretty 154-carat stone, was found!

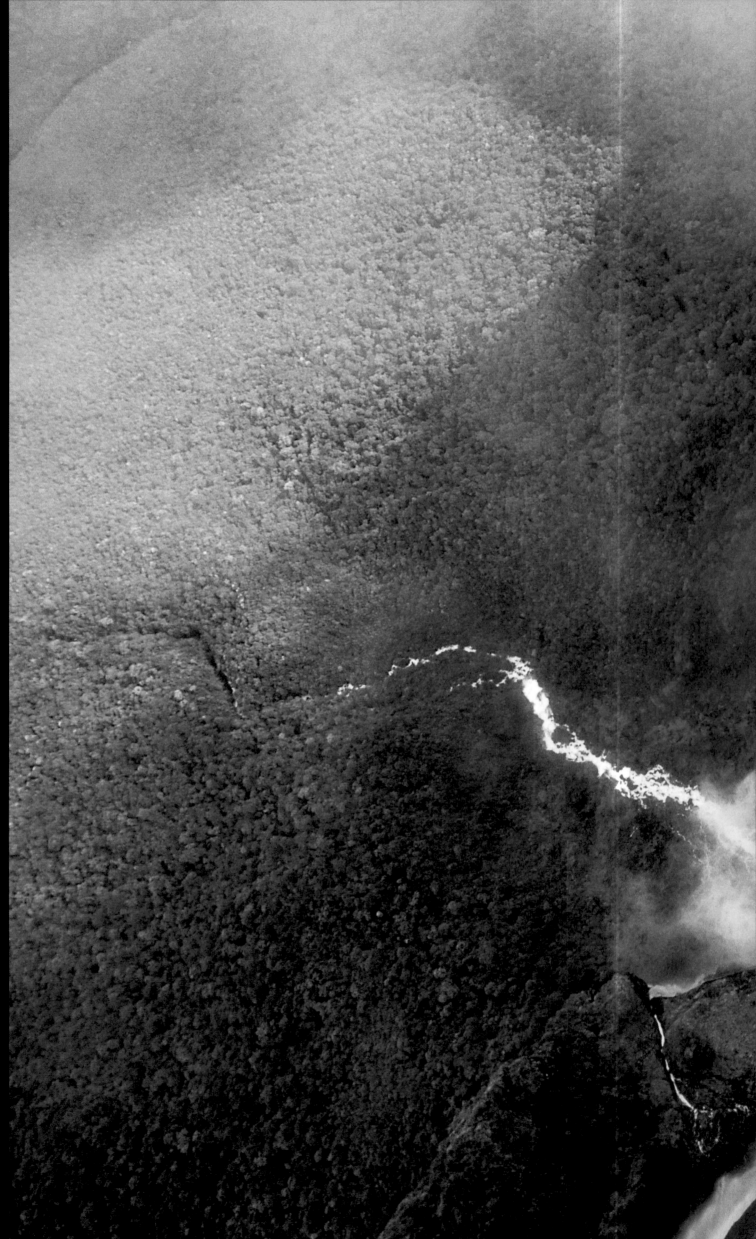

MERINGUES
WHITE DESERT, EGYPT

The white pearl of Egypt is one day's drive away from Cairo, along the Libyan border. An immense desert stretch is punctuated by large rocks as white as snow.

Are genies playing with our senses? The white desert is populated with strange characters: a caped torero, a Mexican wearing his sombrero, a hippopotamus, and even lions taking a nap. It might be that hunger is creating this mirage of scoops of vanilla icecream and other creampuffs. At sunset, these strange monoliths turn into giant candles, which become nearly phosphorescent under the stars. 70 million years ago, the sea covered the region, and when it receded, it left shells and deposited limestone and chalk on the sandstone landscape. Erosion did the rest. Since then, nature puts on a new improvised show every day on this 1,400 square mile stage, depending on the wind and the sand that continue to sculpt and play with the limestone. One day, all of this will disappear and small white pebbles on the sand will be all that remains. People will then know that the genies are back…

A simple Mormon carpenter gave his name to this magnificent natural park, famous for its colored rocks and "fairy chimneys."

Well before the first European explorers in the 18th century and the famous Ebenezer Bryce, man was already living in this part of the Colorado Plateau, tens of thousands of years ago. American Indians were nevertheless wary of the hoodoos, in which they saw evil beings petrified by the gods. The thousands of limestone pinnacles that dominate these vast natural amphitheatres are the result of millennia of erosion. When the sea receded, it left a succession of layers of sediment rich in iron oxide that gives the Canyon its beautiful red color. The altitude of Bryce Canyon, 6,562 to 9,114 feet, ensures both a continental and a mountain climate, particularly rainy in August. Every year, a million tourists visit this 56-square mile natural park, also listed as a national monument, and try to spot the most famous of the many geological structures: Thor's Hammer, E.T. or even Queen Victoria. You need a good eye and a lot of imagination...

HOSTILE MOORLAND
ARAN ISLANDS, IRELAND

On Inishmore, the largest of the Aran Islands, you can walk around all day without ever meeting a soul. Man still chose to settle here!

They tamed this gloomy-looking rock, stacked stones into walls as far as the eye can see and built up a daily routine of agriculture and fishing. Only a few hundred souls still live here at the start of the 21st century, and are rarely bothered by tourists. Lovers of solitude and exciting experiences come to lie face down on the rock, near the edge of the cliff, and look down 300 feet at the waves pounding against the black limestone. These islands are geologically closely related to the Burren, in County Clare, on the west coast of Ireland. A little further along the island, the cliff has dragged down a good part of Fort Aengus in its fall. Considered to be "the most magnificent barbarian monument in Europe" this archeological site (dating from the Iron or Bronze Age) was without a doubt used for religious rather than military purposes. You would not be that surprised to come across a few druids on the heath in the evening at dusk...

40,000 tourists a year come to climb the famous rock every year, whether the Aboriginal people, who venerate this mountain that looms up from the Australian outback, like it or not.

Even stuck right in the middle of the continent-country of Australia, 2,000 miles from Brisbane or Sydney and more than 20 hours by train from Adelaide, Ayers Rock, listed as a UNESCO World Heritage Site, has been a leading tourist attraction for the past 40 years. *Uluru* (its Aboriginal name) is an inselberg or island mountain, the visible part of a subterranean rock formation cleared by erosion. This 1,142-foot high monolith measures 5.8 miles in circumference and reaches 2,831 feet above sea level. Ayers Rock is a sacred site for the Aboriginal people. In the 1980s, the Australian government promised to ban visitors from climbing it but never kept its word. Despite these local traditions, the slope's gradient (up to 60 degrees) and the weather conditions, climbers strive to reach the top to admire the panoramic view and see the rock turn red at sundown.

A SHIVA OF AZURE, GOLD AND SILVER
LAKE TEKAPO, NEW ZEALAND

Tired of carting along so much glacial sediment, Godley River meanders into numerous outstretched arms before flowing into the turquoise waters of Lake Tekapo.

It comes down the 12,316-foot New Zealand Southern Alps full of life, swelled by the ice thaw and carrying with it minerals and micro-organisms. In the sunlight, this glacial or rock "flour" gives its waters, as well as those of Lake Tekapo it flows into, their incredible turquoise blue color. However, the river grows weary on its journey down the mountains and, weighed down by its burden of sand, gravel, mud and sediment, starts to meander and lose its way in one long delta. The river bed has been widening for thousands of years, depositing here and there silt and alluvium, forming shifting landscape features covered in lichen and bushes. Heavy rainfall regularly comes to alter the course of this maze of channels, encroaching ever more on the land. For nature too, life is not always a bed of roses.

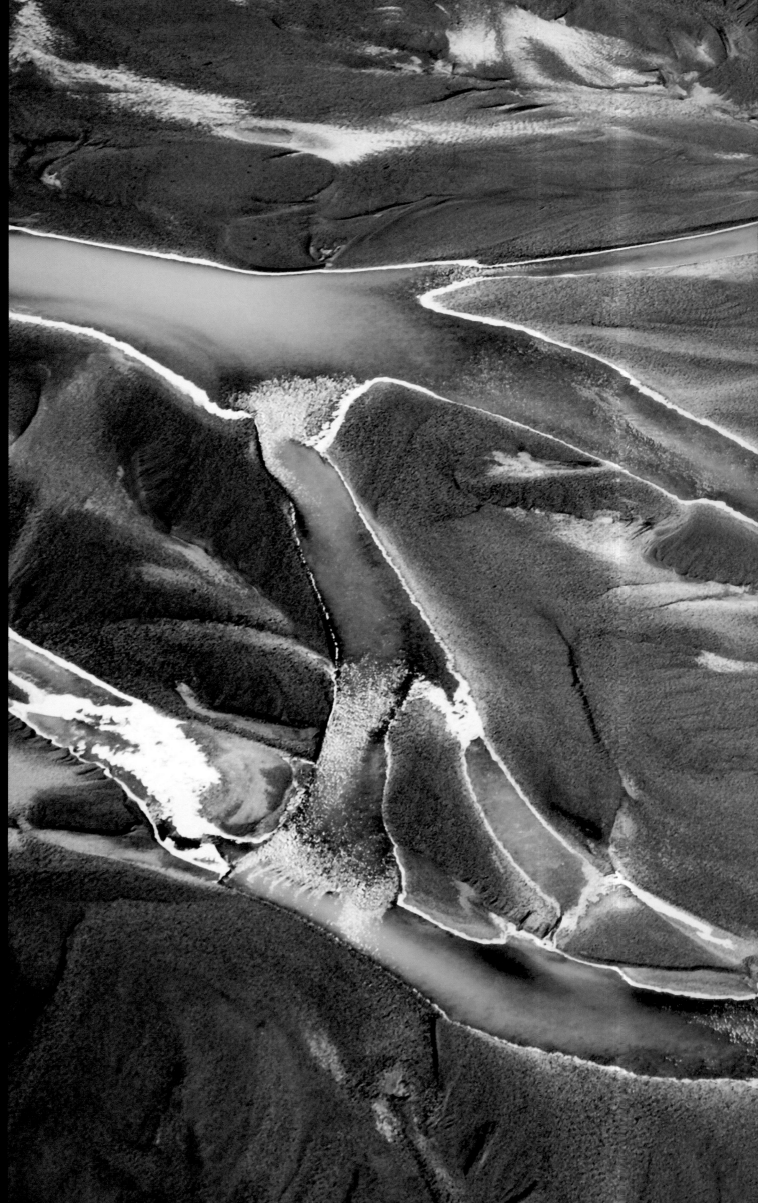

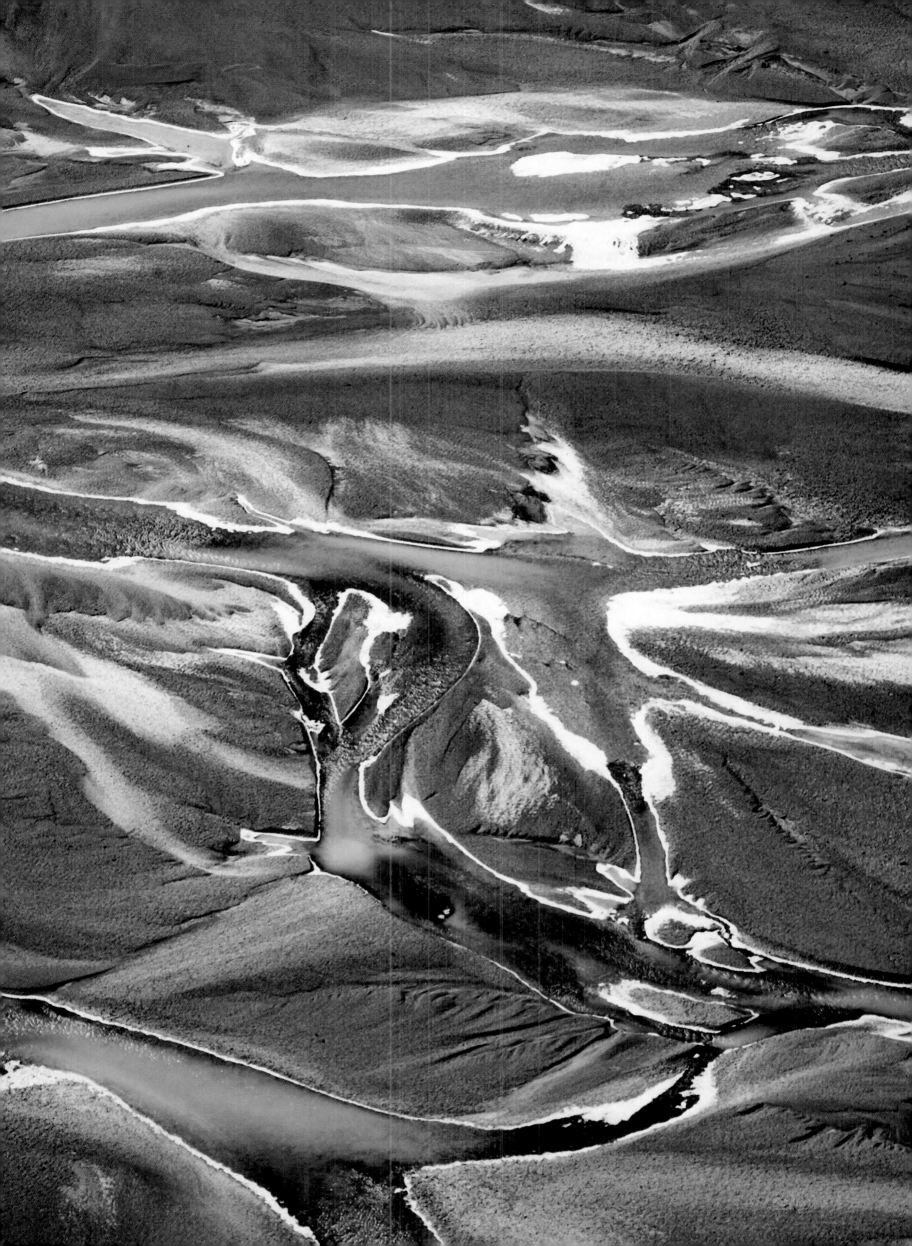

**This giant Italian
icecream turns pink
at sunrise and sunset.
This result of ancient
volcanic activity hides
an incredible troglodyte
habitat.**

It seems hard to imagine
that this lunar valley,
subject to a harsh climate
in the winter, teams with
riches: simple farmers'
houses, rock churches
(365 we are told, one
for each day of the year),
fortresses and even
two underground towns
covering over 1.5 square
miles and seven levels,
which can accommodate
up to 200,000 people.
Before man came along,
erosion also sculpted a
fantastic architecture in
the tuff, a soft rock made
of ashes and mud spewed
out by the volcanoes,
creating domes, gorges
and famous hoodoos
or "fairy chimneys" with
basalt roofs. Impervious to
the huge tourist success
of this UNESCO World
Heritage site, nature
tirelessly continues its
work of destruction and
construction. The dwellings
are strictly monitored to
avoid risk of collapse.
Some peaks are doomed
to disappear whereas
other landscapes are being
hollowed out, proving
that stone houses are not
always a sound long-term
investment…

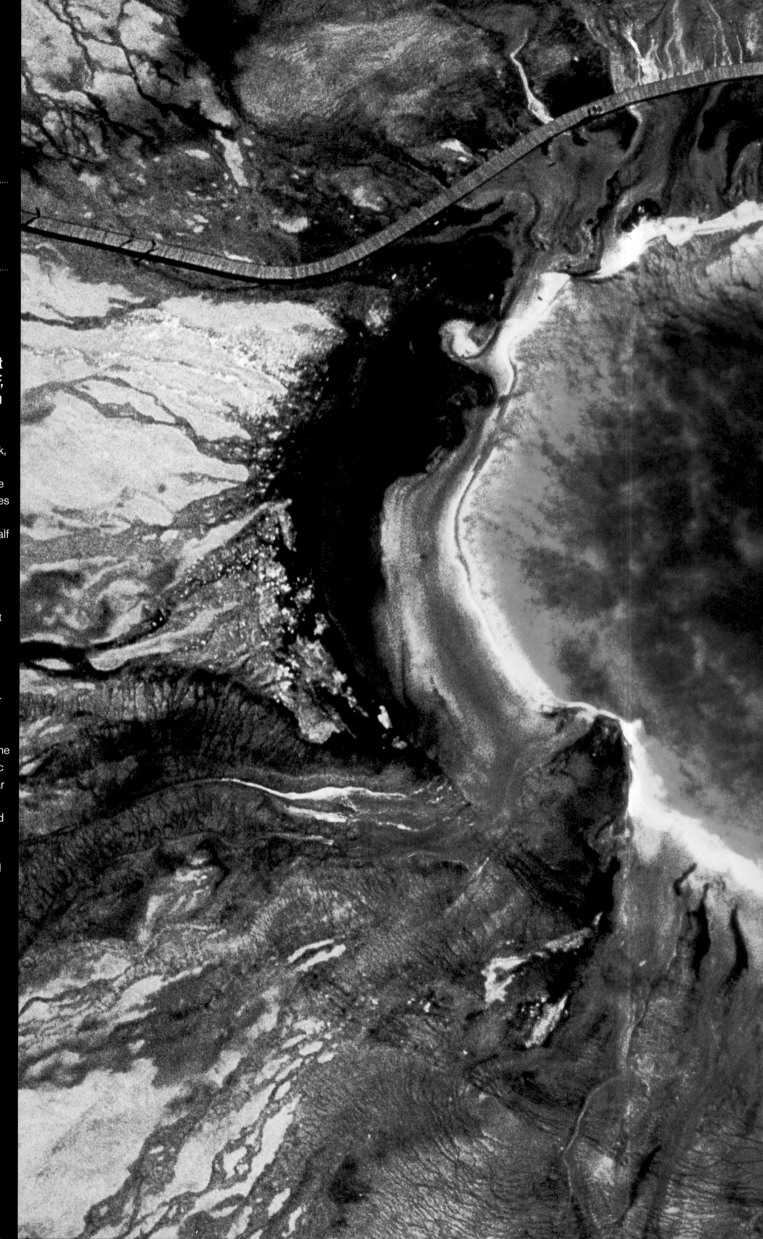

Don't trust the cold colors in this photograph: these are in fact the hottest springs in the world. At a temperature of 158°F, you won't be dipping in your toes...

Yellowstone National Park, a little bigger than twice the surface area of Rhode Island, alone encompasses two thirds of the planet's geysers and more than half the planet's 10,000 hot springs, including the Grand Prismatic. Every minute, more than 560 gallons of boiling hot water come up from the bowels of the earth to fill this 246-foot wide crater. Thermophilic bacteria, a form of primitive life, color these blue, green, and ochre rings, worthy of the most beautiful designs. The site is currently in volcanic and seismic activity similar to that of millions of years ago: the lava accumulated underground swells the earth's crust. In places, the altitude has increased by 2.3 feet in only half a century, that is to say approximately 3 inches per year. New smoke fumaroles are appearing and certain geysers are more active or hotter. The earth is sleeping with one eye open.

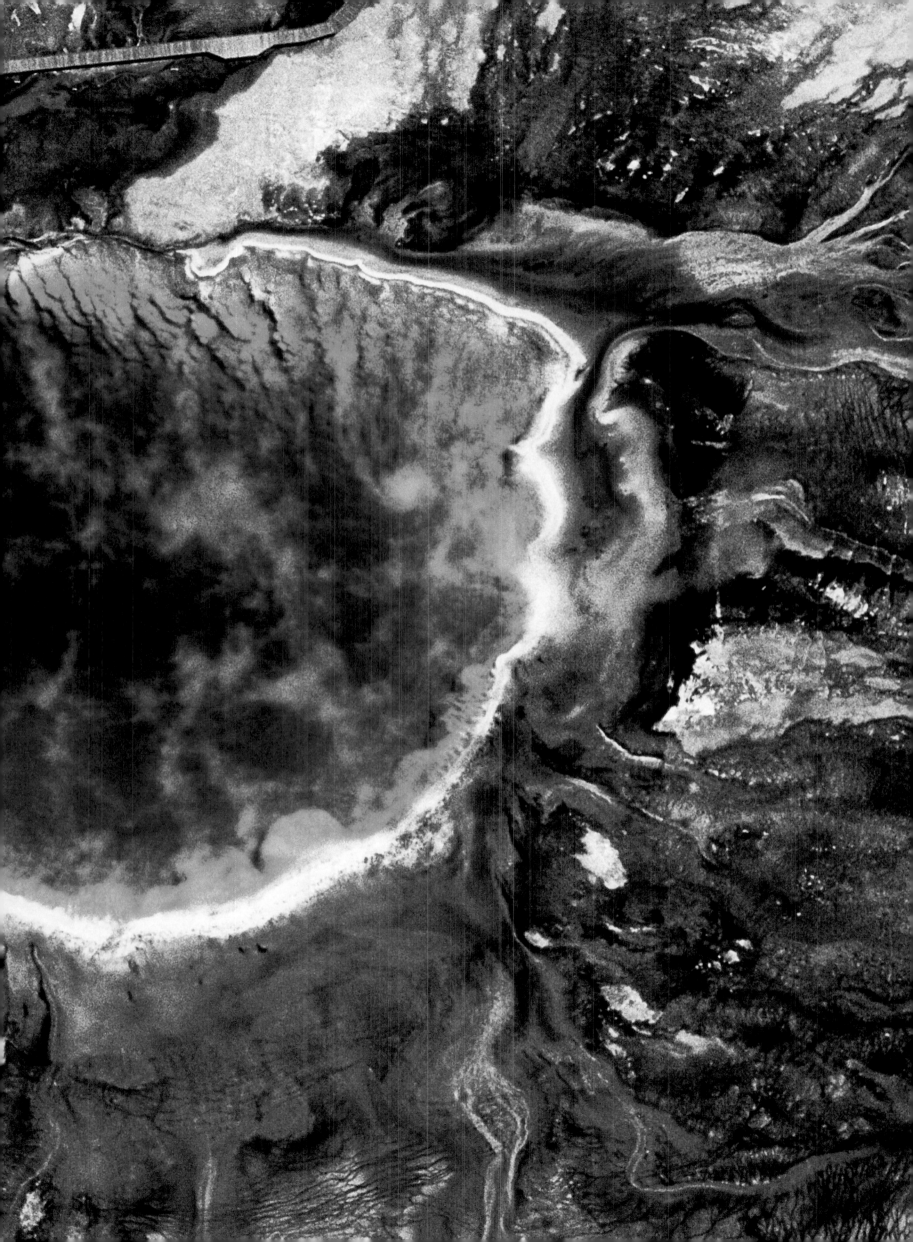

DESERT SHIPWRECK
SHIPROCK, NEW MEXICO,
UNITED STATES

Shiprock is a sacred site for the Navajo Indians. The Westerners see in it the replica of a large 19th century tall ship. What do you think?

Seen from this angle, the Clipper seems ready to pitch, beaten by the rocky waves. It has nevertheless resisted centuries of erosion and wind sculpting the lava core of this extinct volcano, which erupted 30 million years ago. This ghost ship is one of the most unusual sites of the Colorado Plateau and notably in the Four Corners region where the boundaries of the states of Arizona, Colorado, New Mexico and Utah meet at one point. This 1,800-foot jagged volcanic chimney stack can be seen within a 30-mile radius. The rock was climbed for the first time in 1939, an activity later banned in 1970. This sacred Navajo site is said to help raise the human soul above everyday problems.

PRIVATE GULF
NEVERSINK PIT, ALABAMA,
UNITED STATES

To protect this natural well and its endemic species, Neversink Pit was bought up by a cave preservation association.

This 160-foot deep open-air pit is a small world in its own right, with miniature waterfalls, glow-worms, and a rare and endangered species of fern that carpets the walls of the cave. The American philosopher (and amateur botanist) Henry David Thoreau accounted for their presence as a result of the alchemy between the air, limestone and depth of the site. These pits and subterranean caves were formed over millennia by acid rain dissolving certain rocks, and they are typical of the karst landscapes commonly found in the United States. They shelter particularly fragile ecosystems, however, the waters that cross them are often loaded with waste, pesticides and other pollutants. Neversink Pit also became a popular caving site, putting in danger entire populations of bats, contaminated by a mortal virus brought from other caves. That is why the site is now protected and most of it off limits to the public.

CHILDREN'S PAINTINGS
FLY GEYSER, BLACK ROCK DESERT, NEVADA, UNITED STATES

These formations look like sculptures made by children and daubed with paint by small, clumsy hands. This is not so far from the truth: man is indeed behind these strange geysers.

These strange multicolored cones came into being barely one hundred years ago, in 1916. Inhabitants of this arid Nevada region decided to dig a well in the hope of irrigating a few plots of land and watering their cattle. They then fell upon an expanse of water at a temperature of more than 392°F, one among many in the area. The "leak" was reactivated in the 1960s during for more scientific reasons. Another geyser formed and then a third. Boiling jets of water have since escaped, depositing salt and chalky residues all around, forming over time these stalagmites, the oldest measuring up to 13 feet high. These amazing colors are due to thermophilic algae mixed with sediment. If these geysers dried up, the mounds would revert back to grey cones of rock. Water is indeed the element that brings color to life.

HIDE-AND-SEEK
NAKANAI PLATEAU, NEW
BRITAIN ISLAND,
PAPUA NEW GUINEA

This preserved island in the middle of nowhere was populated by headhunters and cannibals less than a century ago. Today, it is particularly renowned for its caves and deep gulfs.

New Britain is a 380-mile long crescent lined with beaches and covered in dense primary forest. The volcanic mountain ranges at the centre of the island still boast half a dozen active craters. The oldest rocks can be found on the Nakanai Plateau, and huge sinkholes – hundreds of feet deep and as many across – have formed in this layer of limestone one mile thick in places, the result of collapsed caves. The most spectacular is the Minye gulf with its 1,535-foot drop, large enough to fit 40,000 Olympic-sized swimming pools. Most of these giant sinkholes hide white water rivers with a staggering flow (up to 700 cubic feet per second), which falls into a network of caves and gigantic underground chambers. Hidden treasures yet to be explored…

The largest salt flat in the world is a coveted site. Multinational companies are fighting over the mineral exploitation rights to gain access to the huge reserves of lithium in the subsoil.

On these high plateaus in southwest Bolivia 12,000 feet above sea level, you have to watch out for optical illusions! The salt desert can turn into a giant mirror in the rainy season, reflecting the sky as far as you can see, and the coral island of Incahuasi, covered in giant cacti, seems to float in the distance on a flying carpet. The Uyuni desert is one of the vestiges of a prehistoric salt water lake that dried up some 40,000 years ago. A little further on, the Laguna Verde and Laguna Colorada owe their names to the minerals that dye their waters green and red. The white desert offers abundant resources: 25,000 tons of salt are extracted every year (a drop in the ocean compared to the estimated 10 billion tons deposited there). It also contains a third of the exploitable lithium sources on the planet. Resisting pressure from battery manufacturers, the Bolivian government has decided to set up its own factory. Too bad for the pink flamingoes that have made this place their home…

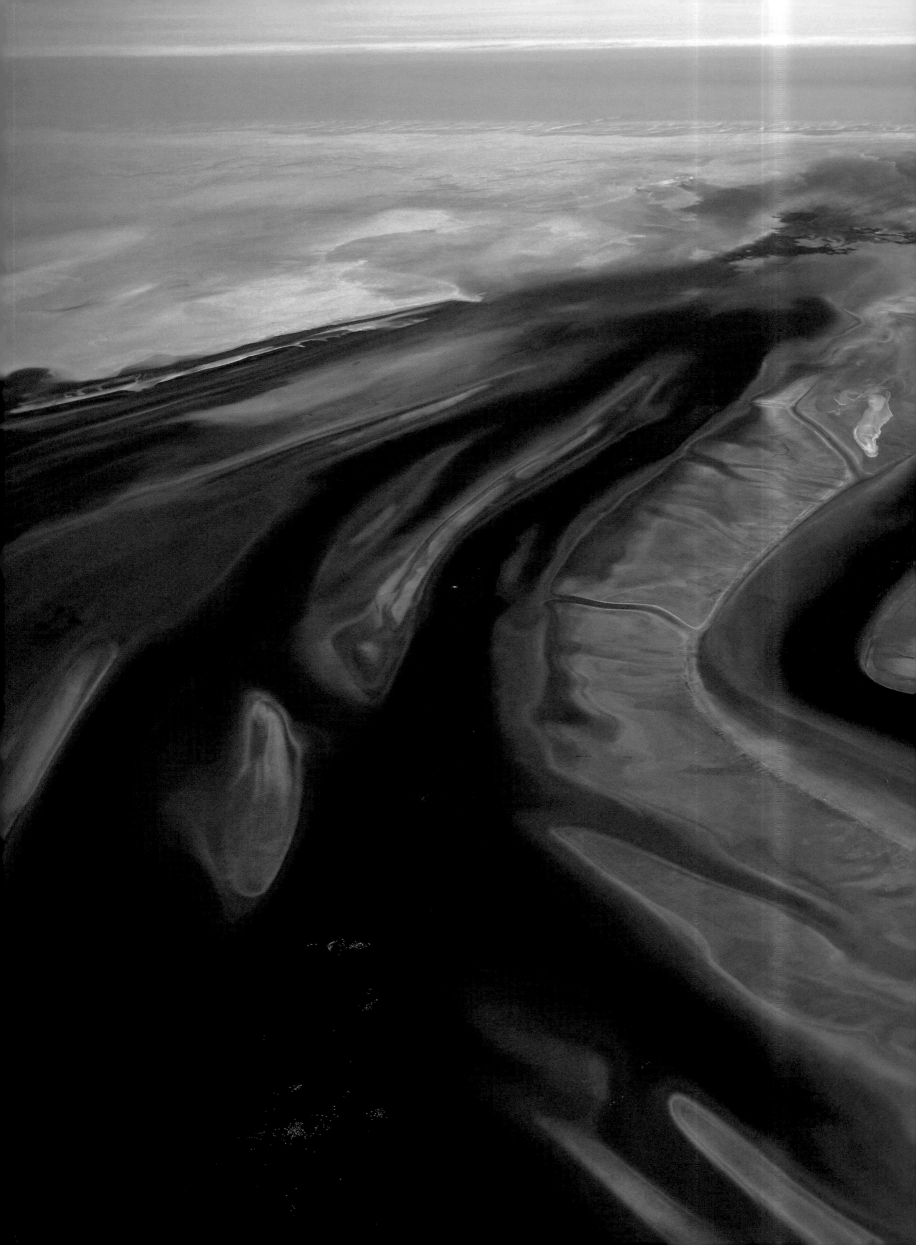

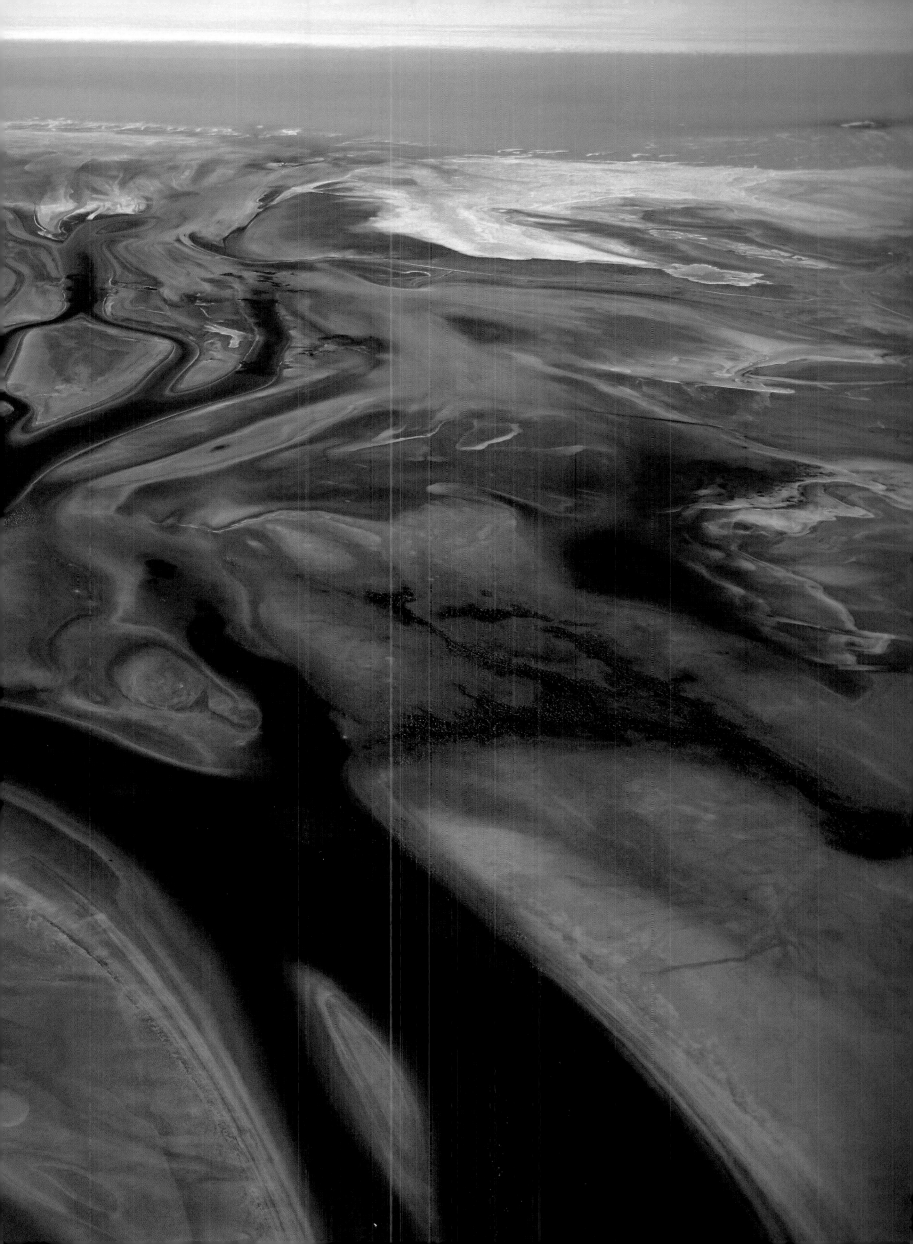

HIBERNATION
BEACON VALLEY, MCMURDO,
ANTARCTICA

In this Antarctic valley of stones, scientists have succeeded in bringing back to life bacteria trapped in the ice for thousands of years.

The "White Continent" is the ideal place for studying the Earth's history and the evolution of life. Antarctica shows strange similarities to polar areas on Mars, but on a smaller scale! Indeed, extra large versions (miles wide) of these curious mosaics of 10-foot volcanic stone can be found on the Red Planet. Beacon is a dry valley, one of the rare unfrozen sites on the Pole. The 190 mile-per-hour winds that sweep Beacon Valley prevent the snow from building up. The extreme temperature variations – a difference of up to 120°F between winter and summer – lead to the formation of cracks in the basalt ground, creating a huge mineral puzzle. Americans and New Zealanders have set up their research stations in the McMurdo region. By bringing back to life frozen bacteria and microbes, they are also looking for proof of the existence of life elsewhere than on the Blue Planet.

CHINESE CURIO
REED FLUTE CAVE, GUILIN,
GUANGXI, CHINA

The entrance to this magical world remained hidden for years behind a hedge of reeds. The Chinese authorities have imagined a somewhat kitsch way of showing off these natural treasures.

Why not a sound and light show amid visitors' exclamations and the multicolored spotlights arranged to give the stalactites, stalagmites and stone columns human, animal or fantasy appearances? This curious site was discovered in 1959, but its inscriptions dating back to the Tang dynasty prove that this cave was known and used from the 7th century onwards. The highlight of the visit is the Dragon King's Crystal Palace, a room that can accomodate to a thousand people. Tourists see a panoramic view of the city of Guilin, reflected at night in the river's waters. 300 million years ago, the Guangxi region, along with a major part of southeast Asia, was under water. Earthquakes and erosion shaped an entire network of caves, stone forests and sugarloaf mountains, making for a guaranteed supernatural sight, both inside and out.

This is one of the most famous scenes in the Southwest, immortalized by more than sixty films and countless advertisements. This vast desert plain is also sacred Navajo territory.

You would hardly be surprised to see John Wayne suddenly appear here on his proud steed and ride out into the sunset. From John Ford Point, such a scene appears in all its familiar glory, including the famous East and West Mittens, Merrick's Butte and the Totem Pole's finger pointing up to the sky. 270 million years ago, Monument Valley was a vast basin, often submerged by water. The sea deposited silt and sediment and the wind added a thick layer of sand snatched from the neighboring mountains. Erosion then shaped these 390- to 1,210-foot-high monoliths, made of more resistant rock and colored by iron oxide and manganese. Various archeological sites have been discovered in the valley, some dating back to 300 years B.C. It is now at the heart of a Navajo Indian reserve, where the tribe has been able to preserve its traditions, language and pastoral way of life, without the cowboys on their heels…

These stepping stones dotted in the Indian Ocean for a giant with seven-league boots may be gobbled up by big bad global warming.

80% of the Maldives' islands are endangered havens. Indeed, the highest peak of this particular coral reef made up of 1,200 stepping stones scattered over 560 miles to the south of Sri Lanka, is no greater than 8 feet above the turquoise sea water. Average temperatures need only increase by 3.6°F and the sea level to rise by 27 inches to see them disappear and turn into a new playground for multicolored fish. Hundreds of thousands of people would then be displaced. With its 400,000 inhabitants, the archipelago, 2.5 times the size of America's capital, is the seventh most densely populated country in the world. The acceleration of coastal erosion and its effects can already be seen. The 2004 tsunami has changed the perimeter of certain islands, and pulverized coral reefs. Despite sea walls being built, ocean remains a threat. Will this paradise still exist for future generations or is it doomed to become a new Atlantis?

THE TREE OF LIFE
FIELDS OF GIANT BAOBAB
TREES, TOLIARA PROVINCE,
MADAGASCAR

Also known as the pharmacy tree, this giant with compact branches is recognizable at first glance and proves very generous to humans.

Everything on the baobab is put to good use! Its fruit, called *pains de singes* ("monkey bread" in French) is as appreciated by humans as it is by primates. Its roasted seeds are a great replacement for coffee. Its pulp mixed with water makes for a refreshing drink. Its leaves are rich in protein and minerals and can cure fevers and diarrhea and protect against malaria. What would we do without it? There are 8 species of baobab including 6 endemic to Madagascar, indeed the best known and most beautiful as well. The island is probably the birthplace of this strange tree, which can be small (10 feet), tall (100 feet) or practically obese (up to 40 feet across) and does not seem to mind growing in a pot as a household plant. Its fibrous wood allows it to store water and get through the dry season. It grows slowly but surely and some specimens are more than 2,000 years old, though thanks to its smooth bark, it is careful never to show its age!

POSEIDON'S ARCH
JURASSIC COAST, DORSET COUNTY, ENGLAND

This perfect arch, worthy of the best stonemasonry, opens out onto the Channel's open water and is the last to survive the erosion nibbling away at the Jurassic Coast cliffs.

From the end of a pebble beach, Durdle Door makes an unusual frame for the spectacular surf. Its name is derived from an Old English word meaning bore or drill. It was indeed hollowed out of the coastline's less resistant strata, taking advantage of a weak point in the rock. The chalk cliffs of the southwest coast of England, known as the Jurassic Coast, were formed 180 million years ago. Rock pinnacles or masses tell us that other similar arches were once dotted along this seafront, before they yielded to the battering waves. The arch's pillars and vault strangely resemble a barn door and are in fact made from different types of limestone. Due to holes left by long-gone vegetation on the upper part of Durdle Door, you could be forgiven for thinking that this edifice was hand built stone upon stone. The light of the setting sun shines golden on this natural architectural formation.

AUTOMATIC SPRINKLER

MOUNT WAI'ALE'ALE, KAUA'I,
HAWAII

If you don't like the rain, just pass on by: Kauai, Hawaii's garden island owes its lush vegetation to Mount Wai'ale'ale, one of the rainiest peaks in the world.

It boasts an average of 36.7 feet of rain per year (20 times more than London) and a record 55.8 feet in 1982. The cause of this weather phenomenon is the green giant that is Wai'ale'ale ("rippling water" in Hawaiian), an extinct volcano reaching 5,148 feet at its highest peak, which attracts clouds from the north and east and concentrates this precipitation on its steep slopes. Its summit is often hidden in mist; rivers and cascades run down its sides and have sculpted the landscape over the centuries, slowly but surely hollowing out Waimea Canyon, the largest in the Pacific Ocean. The old caldera, at 3,937 feet, is home to wetlands, the natural sanctuary for endemic bird species and rare plants. The vegetation is dense and omnipresent wherever you look and the slow erosion of volcanic rock has created spectacular natural decors. These magnificent landscapes have been used as a backdrop for more than 70 Hollywood films. King Kong and Indiana Jones are not going to be put off by a few bucketfuls of water!

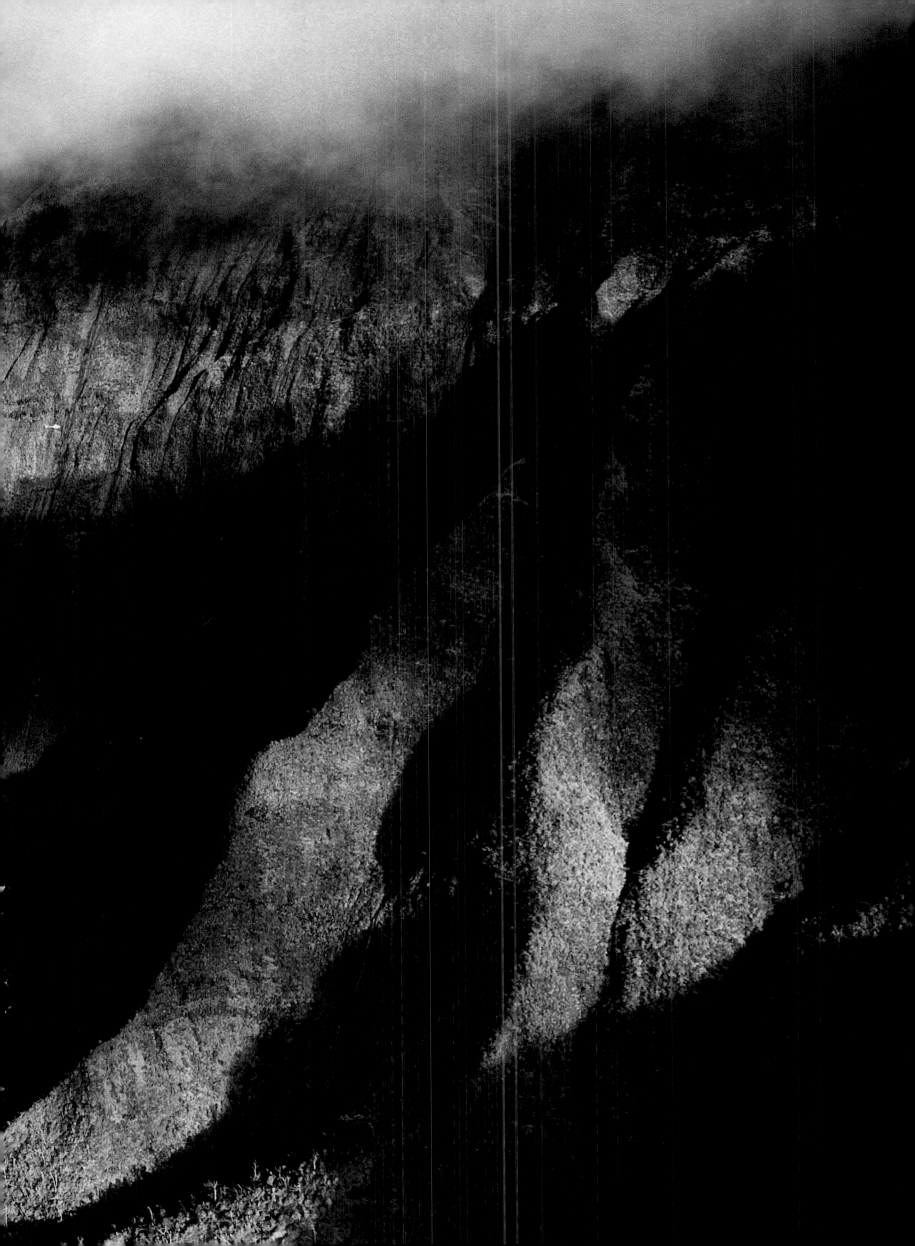

GALE FORCE 7
CLIGGA HEAD, CORNWALL,
ENGLAND

Off the coast of Cornwall, there is electricity in the... water! The United Kingdom – among others – is working on the Wavehub project aiming to use the power of the waves.

Cornwall has had to learn to come to terms with the changing moods of the sea, whether it brought pirates of yesteryear, French "johnnies" arriving to sell their onions or even surfers who come to court the waves. Tomorrow Cornwall may become the home of installations for the Wavehub project. Indeed, the English are making progress in this innovative renewable energy concept. And this should make a few waves in this sardine-fishing county. The area surrounding Cligga Head was for a long time a land of tin and copper mines. The granite cliffs still bear the scars of this activity, with scattered signs of tunnels and galleries so popular now with cavers. This English county is sometimes confused with Cornouaille in Brittany, France, no doubt because of their common Celtic origins.

ROOTS AND STONE
NAMBUNG NATIONAL PARK, AUSTRALIA

If the builders of Stonehenge had travelled the world, they would have left a few megaliths in these dunes, located not far from Perth, in Western Australia.

This desert of Pinnacles is littered with thousands of limestone concretions of different shapes and sizes. The stromatolites (rocky cauliflower-shaped masses) and natural standing stones that can reach up to 13 feet high have often been compared to tombstones, fingers or termites' nests. During the Quaternary Period, thick vegetation covered the ground. Columns of calcareous sandstone gradually formed around the deepest roots. With climate change, the region became a desert and erosion shaped these underground concretions. Despite the harsh conditions, plants remain very much a part of the landscape. Wild flowers grow from the sand in the spring. The fauna tends to be nocturnal, but you often come across Grey Kangaroos during the day. The sight is at its most unique at dawn and dusk, when these megaliths cast their ghostly shadows over the dunes.

POLAR BLANKETS
WRANGELL-ST. ELIAS
NATIONAL PARK, ALASKA,
UNITED STATES

This "mountain kingdom" is difficult to outshine since it is the biggest national park in the United States, with the highest peaks, and an incalculable number of glaciers.

Located in an international biosphere reserve, this park is larger than nine U.S. states. It is home to 9 of the 16 highest peaks in the United States and more than 150 glaciers, including the Hubbard that advances approximately 30 feet every day. A multitude of rivers and streams flow down from these seas of ice, swelling when the snows finally melt. Indeed in this near-coastal region, the ocean's moderating influence is halted by the mountains and the fields of ice. Winters are long and harsh. The vegetation can vary depending on the thickness and depth of the permafrost (which develops when the ground remains frozen two years or more). There are expanses of tundra, peat bogs and swamps as well as taiga (also known as boreal forests), with a mixture of conifers, aspens, birches, willows and spruce… This is the land of moose, caribou and grizzlies! Not so surprising if you bear in mind the quantities of tender lichen and the salmon-filled rivers.

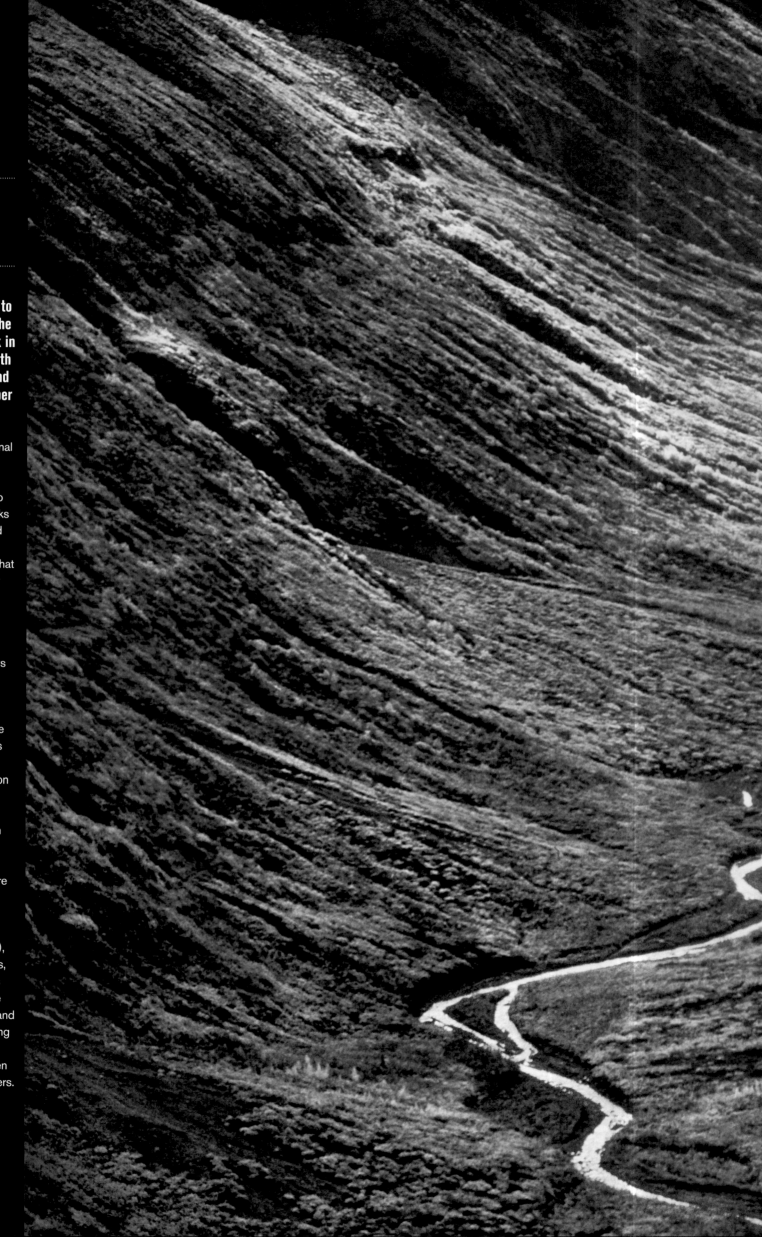

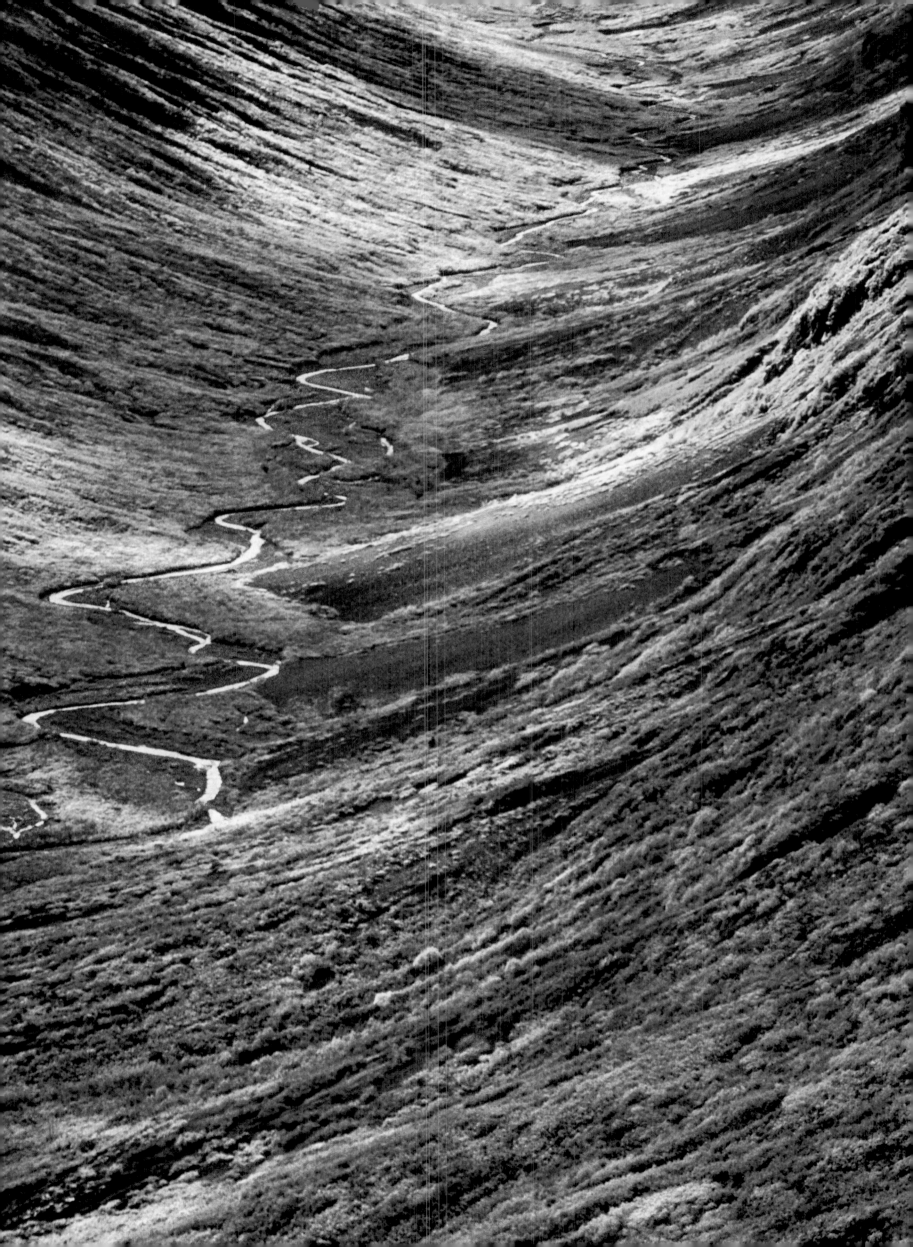

THE FAKIR'S BED
TSINGY DE BEMARAHA
NATURE RESERVE,
MADAGASCAR

Seen from above, this vast network of faults looks like a carpet of formidable prickly spikes. Once used as shelter, these calcareous cathedrals are now a place of worship.

In Malagasy, Tsingy means "where you cannot walk barefoot." These unique and ragged mountain ranges appeared following the movement of tectonic plates as the island of Madagascar broke away from the African continent. These limestone rocks are made of fossils and shellfish that died in the sea 200 million years ago, sculpted by the rain into sharp blades and needles. Their fairly complex hydrology enables the Tsingy to act as water towers for the region. This mineral world stretches out over more than 370,000 acres and is the largest protected site in Madagascar. It is surrounded by savannah and dry forest populated with baobabs and commiphora, a very resilient tree, highly prized by carpenters and used for its resin and golden parchment-like bark. And, like the Tsingy, some varieties also come with large prickles.

SERIAL FALLS
IGUAÇU FALLS,
ARGENTINA / BRAZIL

A gem hidden in an exceptional showcase of greenery, this massive wall of water is nothing short of an awesome sight. Brazil and Argentina are contenders for the best vantage point to admire this natural wonder.

Both the falls and their environment make this site nestled in the 45,000 acre cross-border natural park an exceptional place. Right in the middle of the tropical forest, 275 waterfalls stretch out over a 2-mile front, plunging from an average height of 262 feet. This is due to the Iguaçu River's sudden drop, falling straight down the basalt cliffs. The 300-foot Devil's Throat is without a doubt the most spectacular part with its 14 horseshoe-shaped cataracts. No less than 460,000 cubic feet of water flow out of it every second in a muffled roar, and thick mists are known to produce huge rainbows. You also have to decide from where to admire this sight. On the Brazilian side, various facilities enable you to get a panoramic view; head for Argentina for a cozier vantage point. You might be lucky enough to spot toucans, parrots or eagles flying over the falls.

AT THE MOVIES
PARIA RIVER VALLEY, ARIZONA, UNITED STATES

....

Paria Canyon puts on no less than a full Technicolor show, particularly in the low-angled light at the end of the day. All that is missing is Hollywood cowboys.

In the days of black and white pictures, the first westerns were already being filmed here, leaving movie lovers completely in the dark as to the colorful sight that they were missing: cliffs in hues of red, orange, purple, grey and white that 30 to 40 million years of erosion have sculpted into amazing shapes patterned with stylistic scrolls and regular grooves. The Paria River (Pahreah is Native American for "muddy waters") also played a part in this work. This fickle watercourse is the main affluent in Colorado between Lake Powell and the Grand Canyon. It winds through narrow gorges such as Buckskin Gulch: like a tiny ant at the foot of these thousand-foot-tall rock faces, walkers can touch both sides, with arms outstretched. However, watch out for those storms! In next to no time, the river that is practically dry in places can quickly turn into a torrent of mud, sweeping along rocks and tree trunks. Movie stars are often temperamental.

The United States sees a record-breaking number of tornadoes every year, especially in certain Southern states. In the spring, the air has a tendency to blow hot and cold.

Texas, Oklahoma, Nebraska, Kansas and Missouri are collectively nicknamed "Tornado Alley." 700 to 1,200 tornadoes are recorded every year, in particular when fine weather days return in the spring and summer. Peak activity has been noted in the month of May, when cold air currents from the Pole clash with hot air currents coming up from the Gulf of Mexico. The whirlwinds generated by this strong difference in temperature are accompanied by exceptionally violent winds. These can turn into dry tornadoes or "dust devils," carting off dirt, dust and debris in their path. The great desert plains are also particularly important breeding grounds for sand tornadoes, where you can often see a number of whirlwinds following each other in single file. These corridors of destruction generally keep to a straight course and beyond this apocalyptic path – as strange as it may seem – all is calm!

HOT WATER ON TAP
THINGVELLIR NATIONAL PARK,
ICELAND

Whether it falls from the sky or gushes out of the ground icy cold or hot, water is everywhere in Iceland. This geologically young land is still in formation thanks to its permanent volcanic activity.

This island very much deserves its name of the land of ice: indeed, 10% of its surface is covered with glaciers, including the largest in Europe, the Vatnajökull. Volcanic activity causes constant and rapid changes across the ages. In the Southwest, past earthquakes have created a vast trough fault with multiple rifts in part covered by Lake Thingvellir, now home to various species of fish that are unique in the world. When the magma teems under the Earth's crust, natural pools and the river's waters meandering to the lake see their temperatures increase, geysers explode and cauldrons of mud make enormous bubbles. This mix of water and fire is used to produce geothermal and hydraulic energy. Despite these "eco-friendly" efforts, Icelanders produce four times more greenhouse gases per inhabitant than the French, for example, in large part due to car-related pollution.

ICEBERG FACTORY
ICEFIELD, WEDDELL SEA, ANTARCTIC

Many expeditions have lost the fight hook, line and sinker! This is one of the planet's most formidable seas with some of the worst sailing conditions. In some places, the ice floe covering the water is more than 16,000-foot-deep.

Today, even icebreakers steer clear of this part of the Southern Ocean, which extends 1.1 million square miles. The Weddel Sea has the coldest ocean waters on Earth and carries along gigantic blocks of ice that break away from the Larsen, Ronne and Filchner ice shelves. Indeed, ship captains try to avoid being crushed by the ice field, like the fate of a number of scientific research boats of yesteryear, including Ernest Shackleton's infamous Endurance. During the austral winter, the ice doubles the continent's surface area and yet, Antarctica, a colossal supply of fresh water for the planet, lies just below the hole in the ozone layer which makes it particularly vulnerable to global warming. The annual thaw has increased twenty times between 2002 and 2009, unexpectedly freeing near the surface hundreds of species still unknown by scientists.

HIDDEN TREASURE
GOBI DANXIA PARK, GANSU PROVINCE, CHINA

Man has explored space and walked on the moon but he is far from having unearthed all of the treasures on the Blue Planet: these multicolored mountains were only discovered in 2005!

Today, tourists flood in from all over the world to admire these "red mountains" covered in vegetation and surrounded by rivers, and which turn even redder after the rain. Danxia means "pink cloud" in Mandarin, a poetic name for these reddish limestone formations eroded over time, resulting in these unusual rocks and series of mountains surrounded by curved cliffs. These mountains were a longstanding secret even though they cover an area of 180 square miles in the Gansu province. Similar landscapes can be found in other regions of southern China (Hunan, Zhejiang, Jiangxi, Fujian, Guizhou and Guangdong). Local authorities have not hesitated to move populations and to ban tree-felling in order to preserve the sites. Indeed, China is proud of these treasures and has asked for these mountains to be listed as a UNESCO World Heritage Site.

El Tatio is the largest geyser field in the Southern Hemisphere. It stretches out over 8 square miles at the heart of the Atacama salt flat, 14,173 feet above sea level.

This landscape is truly magical at daybreak. The cold air in the early hours makes the site's 80 active geysers more vigorous. Their fumaroles, which on average measure 2.5 to 3.3 feet, can be as large as 30 feet and reach temperatures of 185°F. This sight is fleeting and comes to an end as soon as the first rays of sun are felt. The Atacama *salar* (saline deposit) then appears in its mineral immensity, like a white sea, with its salt crust and chaotic shapes, its petrified wavelets and ground cracked by the heat. The air is so dry that mists never disrupt the landscape, offering uninterrupted views of the 150 square miles all the way to the Licancabur and Lascar volcanoes. Core drilling has shown that the salty crust is dozens of feet thick in places. We now know that 10,000 years are needed to obtain a few inches of salt deposit, making Atacama the oldest salt desert in the world.

SEA OF SAND
SOSSUSVLEI, NAMIB DESERT,
NAMIBIA

The planet's oldest
desert covers more than
30,000 square miles and
is home to 1000-foot
dunes, the highest in
the world. Despite the
blazing heat, there are
signs of life.

The Sossusvlei lies along
the Atlantic coast and
is the most accessible
part of the Namib Desert.
It is known for its huge
orangey-red dunes and
its numerous dried-up
basins littered with dead
trees, such as the Dead
Vlei clay pan. These iron
oxide-colored sands were
brought millions of years
ago by easterly winds,
sometimes from as far as
the Kalahari. The region's
arid conditions are older
still, since an old petrified
desert forms sandstone
bedrock under the dune
fields. Nevertheless, this
sea of sand is far from
uninhabited. The Benguela
Current, cooled by the
Atlantic, enables mists to
form a sufficient supply of
life-giving humidity. Despite
the ground temperature
rising up to 158°F, animals
are able to find a cool
spot under the sand.
Small lakes develop in
the summer when it rains,
and hordes of birds come
to frolic and admire the
reflection of the red dunes.

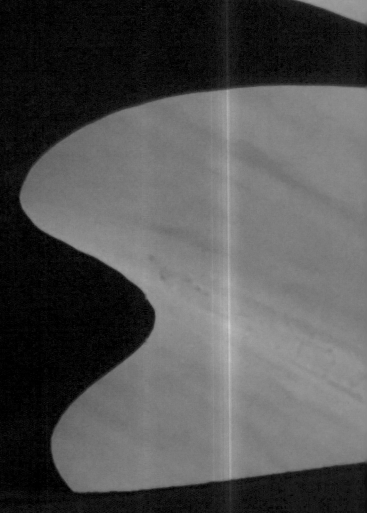

THE MOUNTAIN OF GOD
OL DOINYO LENGAI VOLCANO,
NGORONGORO CRATER,
TANZANIA

Ol Doinyo Lengai Volcano's huge crater is the only volcano to release special natro carbonatite lava.

The Ol Doinyo volcano's symmetric cone reaches more than 3,000 feet above the Gregory Rift Valley and towers above Lake Natron, which it feeds in soda ash. Ol Doinyo Lengai is the Maasai population's sacred volcano and home to their supreme god Ngai. In this flat-bottomed basin, measuring 12 miles across and 2,000 feet deep, special carbonate-rich carbonatite lava is released at relatively low temperatures (914 to 1,004°F). This lava is extremely fluid (even more than the Hawaiian lava) and its ebony color turns brown then snowy white hue in the 2 to 3 following days… To preserve the site (and the Maasai tribes), a vast 3,000-square mile conservation area has been created.

THE GIANT PANDA BATH
HUANGLONG, SICHUAN, CHINA

The water in these natural pools is crystal-clear, but only the Giant Panda and other endangered species in this valley in Sichuan are allowed to bathe in it!

The name of this valley, Huanglong, comes from its supposed ressemblance to a huge listless dragon of yellow stone, stretching out over two and half miles at the outermost bounds of China, near the border with Tibet. The national park consists of numerous unique landscapes, 5,577 to 18,268 feet above sea level. On its highest peak, more than 3,400 small overflow pools full of perfectly pure and translucent water ripple against the side of the mountain. These natural ponds were formed over thousands of years by an accumulation of calcite deposits, which give them their exceptional and ever-changing colors. Seen from the sky, they look like a giant mosaic. The Chinese authorities keep a close eye on this UNESCO World Heritage Site: it is strictly forbidden to venture off the marked footpaths and disturb the Giant Pandas, Asian Black Bears or the Golden Snub-nosed Monkeys, which come down from the snowy peaks to enjoy the hot springs and these heavenly pools.

A RIVER RUNS THROUGH IT

OFAERUFOSS FALLS, ELDGJA VALLEY, ICELAND

The Eldgja volcanic canyon in the southeast of Iceland is the largest in the world. At the bottom of this "fire canyon" flows the Ofaerufoss waterfall.

A gigantic volcanic eruption gave birth 2,000 years ago to this huge fault in the high plateaus of southern Iceland, measuring 19 miles long, 1,300 feet wide and 460 feet deep. A river now runs through it down a double waterfall, cascading off a number of levels. The site is not free from the Earth's terrible whims, so frequent in Iceland. In 1783, for example, the neighboring volcano woke up with a violent start. Its 135 craters projected 500 billion cubic feet of lava, ash, and toxic gases that led to famine and poisonings. The poor harvest in France that led to the revolution a few years later was even blamed on this cataclysm. As recently as twenty years ago, an earthquake destroyed the charming natural lava bridge that crossed the Ofaerufoss falls. It is frequently replaced by a rainbow, when the water takes the time to play with the light.

SUPER-DELTA
ISHKOWIK RIVER, YUKON-KUSKOKWIM DELTA, ALASKA

With the return of spring, the largest delta in North America is a unique haven for birds. The winter, however, is much harsher for the humans who have chosen to live there.

Land surrounded by water on all sides and as far as the eye can see! The Yukon-Kuskokwim Delta is one of the largest in the world. The huge alluvial plain, a mosaic of lakes, swamps, rivers and streams, is for the most part covered in tundra. The 30,000-square-mile natural reserve sees thousands of swans, geese and ducks arrive in the spring to seek shelter and feed in these damp prairies. The delta is home to approximately 20,000 inhabitants, mainly Native Americans and Eskimos, divided up between the town of Bethel and approximately 50 villages cut off from the world for most of the year. There are no roads here, so boats are the only means of travel in the summer while snowmobiles and dogsleds are used when the rivers are frozen. The poorest still live off hunting and the food they gather. Jack London described Alaska as "a country where whiskey freezes solid and may be used as a paper-weight for a large part of the year."

FIRE AND ICE
MYRDALSJÖKULL GLACIER
AND KATLA VOLCANO,
ICELAND

Under this huge 230-square-mile icecap lays one of the most active volcanoes in Iceland. When it awakes, it provokes devastating floods.

Iceland is sitting on a powder keg. Located at the edge of the European and American plates, the island has more than 130 volcanoes, including the violent Katla (4,961 feet) that erupts an average of two times per century. It is capped with a large white hat, the Mýrdalsjökull or "Mire Dale Glacier" in Icelandic, which is slowly making its way towards the Atlantic, with a varying thickness of 650 to 2,300 feet depending on the spot. A reservoir of magma can be found two miles under the Mýrdalsjökull, and the heat of the molten lava melts the lower layers of ice. When the temperature rises considerably, an ice disaster takes place – as was the case in 1918 – leading to a ten- to hundred-fold increase in flow and a powerful flood laying waste to the surrounding plains. This union of opposites is particularly feared by the Icelanders, always ready to flee if fire and ice unleash their powers.

SUGAR LOAFS
GUIZHOU AND GUANGXI
PROVINCES, CHINA

Whether mirrored in the waters of the Li River or surrounded with terraced rice fields or rape fields, these rounded hills are typical of the southwest region of China.

These are the "forgotten" provinces, long isolated due to their rugged mountainous landscape and the late arrival of the railroad. Their inhabitants are predominantly farmers, and tourism is far less developed than in neighboring Yunnan. These beautiful landscapes have therefore been perfectly preserved. The region abounds in forests and hidden caves, hollowed out by water over the millennia. Let's not forget the famous "Dragon's Teeth," the name given by the Chinese to these eroded hills, similar to those found in Ha Long Bay and characteristic of karst landscapes. 300 million years ago, the sea covered a major part of the Middle Kingdom. When it receded, it left a thick layer of limestone. Earthquakes and erosion then shaped this into spectacular features. The vegetation is lush everywhere thanks to a humid climate, and the province of Guizhou is also home to the Huangguoshu waterfalls, the largest in Asia.

A VISION OF PARADISE
BORA BORA ISLAND, FRENCH POLYNESIA

This Eden floating on turquoise waters barely measures 15 square miles. A coral necklace protects this old volcano, which sunk into the Pacific.

Bora Bora... its name alone, a distortion of Pora Pora, meaning "first born" in Tahitian, is enough to get the imagination going. The island is said to have been created by the god Taaroa just after the island of Raiatea. It emerged from the waters 13 million years ago, and the highest of its three mounts culminates at only 2,385 feet. The old volcano gradually sunk into the sea, giving birth to a lagoon encircled by a barrier reef and large enough in places to support a string of *motu*, small islands of sand and coral debris. Three bays open up onto the lagoon, including Tuuraapuo, to the west, made up of an old, now submerged, crater. Directly opposite, Teavanui Channel is large enough for boats to pass through and is the island's only opening onto the ocean. The landing strip, dating from the last world war, was for years the longest in Polynesia. This is one of the vestiges of the presence of American troops; this paradise was once a wartime military base.

In Hobart, it is simply called "the mountain,"and its landscapes, panoramic view and blanket of snow are indeed unique.

Mount Wellington is often mistakenly thought to be an extinct volcano. The upper part of the 4170-foot peak results from an impact that took place 40 million years ago, when the Australian continent broke away from Antarctica, leaving Tasmania, an island as big as one and a half times the state of Hawaii, in its wake. A layer of ebony-colored solidified magma then slid in among the older rock. The mountain's core is made up of marine deposits accumulated during the period when the Hobart plain was under water. Its slopes gradually became covered with dense forests. A little further up, Sphinx Rock reveals impressive dolerite columns known as the Organ Pipes and much appreciated by climbers. Another unusual feature in this landscape is the Octopus Tree, a huge tree that winds its roots around large rocks. Quite often, and even in the summer, the summit of Mount Wellington, scoured by the wind, is covered in snow.

HYPERACTIVE
MOUNT ETNA, SICILY

After nearly one hundred eruptions in a century, Etna is surely one of the most active volcanoes in the world and continues to fascinate scientists.

Also called *Mongibello* (the "Mountain of Mountains"), this 300,000 year old volcano towers above the east coast of Sicily. Its top is 10,974 feet above sea level, with a base 28 miles in diameter. It is most of the time crowned with a large white cloud of steam and gas, or ashes during eruptions. Its intense activity makes it one of the greatest volcanoes of the decade with experts from the world over coming to its bedside as soon as it starts spitting out fire. This phenomenon can either be explained by the explosions from any of its four craters or to outpourings from the fissures found along the volcano's slopes. The highly liquid lava flows sometimes reach the Mediterranean Sea to form features such as the famous Cyclopean Isles, swallowing up houses and even villages on their way. Eruptions make colorful and smoky sights, and such was the case during the eruption of Mount Pinatubo in the Philippines in June 1991 (overleaf).

MARSH LILIES
PANTANAL PARK, MATO GROSSO, BRAZIL

The Pantanal, a huge marsh for six months of the year, is the planet's largest wetlands and boasts a particularly complex ecosystem.

This area of the Mato Grosso (literally "thick jungle") is often eclipsed by the Amazonian rainforest, at the heart of all conservationists' concerns. The marsh is nevertheless very fragile and has in turn fallen victim to deforestation, intensive agriculture and pesticides. The Pantanal is home to a great variety of animals and the richest collection of aquatic plants in the world. Indeed, 80% of its 77,000 square miles are underwater most of the year, the sea being so close and the altitude so low; both favor water stagnation. This being said, the marsh dries up completely when the rainy season is over. The tropical climate encourages the development of surprising plants such as the giant water lily. Its round "cake tin" leaves grow up to 10 feet across and it colonizes stretches of water, producing beautiful but fleeting white flowers in the summer.

SACRED WHITE
BAISHUI TERRACES, YUNNAN PROVINCE, CHINA

The largest limestone terraces in China are a tourist attraction, but more importantly a place of pilgrimage, since they are the cradle of the Dongba religion.

They look like white marble, but these terraces located at 7,808 meters above sea level in the mountainous northwest province of Yunan, are in fact made of high-density calcium carbonate sediment. Brought by the spring water from the mountains, it has accumulated over hundreds of thousands of years to form these immaculate steps. This exceptional site stretches out over 1.2 square miles and 328 feet in height, and brings to mind the terraced rice fields so frequently found in the region. These pure white geological formations mirror the sun and, with the snowy peaks of Mount Yulongxue (18,360 feet) as a backdrop, form the ideal site for a sanctuary. According to legend, the founder of the Dongba culture settled here on his return from Tibet, to spread his faith. For a religion that venerates the color white and preaches harmony between man and nature, it would be hard to find a better place…

POLAR HALLUCINATIONS
AURORA BOREALIS, ALASKA,
UNITED STATES

The sky and sun entertain us with their dance of the seven veils, making for a colorful show called the aurora borealis in the Northern Hemisphere and the aurora australis in the Southern Hemisphere.

This practically daily light phenomenon is primarily observed in Greenland, Alaska, in the north of Canada and in Antarctica. The towns of Fairbanks and Nome witness count approximately 200 of them every year. These colorful veils of green, blue and red are sometimes visible far from the Poles. Indeed, the inhabitants of Honolulu in 1859 and Singapore in 1909 thought they were hallucinating! The polar auroras are the result of emissions of atoms and subatomic particles by the sun. When they arrive in the atmosphere, they excite oxygen and nitrogen atoms that suddenly set the sky ablaze for a few minutes and sometimes for a number of hours. Space exploration has enabled us to find out more about this phenomenon, including the fact that Jupiter and Saturn also have polar auroras. In 1975, the Franco-Russian program Araks even succeeded in recreating an artificial aurora.

IN THE SORCERER'S CAULDRON
DANAKIL DESERT, ETHIOPIA

Something is bubbling in this Ethiopian volcano's cooking pot! The lava lakes are stirred by waves and bubbles that cast up magma at more than 1800°F.

The Erta Ale (2,011 feet) has fascinated scientists with its eruption activity. It is one of only three volcanoes in the world to have at its peak a caldera with two craters in the shape of round wells, the site of permanent lava lakes. We are here at the origins of the Earth, at the heart of a very active seismic and volcanic area, as well as on the edge of three rifts (downfaulting of the Earth's crust). The Erta Ale is part of a string of volcanoes that stretches out over 60 miles, in the Danakil Depression, a barren valley once covered by the sea and now famous for being one of the hottest and most inhospitable areas on the planet. These places are nevertheless full of a certain kind of poetry, as is the case with acid lakes such as Dallol, colored in yellow, green, or orange by record levels of sulfur. The high salt, magnesium chloride, potassium and brine content have created numerous concretions resembling salt crystals, mushrooms, eggshells or porous sponges, a phenomenon accentuated by high temperatures (often rising above 122°F) and the absence of wind. This landscape is as vicious as it is bewitching.

Very transient flashes of lightning during a volcanic eruption are known to have provoked fires in surrounding forests.

Scientists are very much aware of these volcanic storms even though they have rarely been studied. During an eruption, large electrically-charged volcanic plumes appear and can be mistaken for storm cumulonimbus. Particles expelled from the crater rub against each other and produce flashes of lightning at the peak of volcanic activity. Large sparks and upward-surging flashes of lightning coming directly from the volcano's crater have been more recently observed. These remain very similar to lightning produced by storms, and during this period, thunder can also be heard. The power of such phenomena is of course linked to the eruption's force and the type of volcano. It has been noted that red volcanoes, such as those in Hawaii, which only belch out lava flows, do not produce flashes of lightning, making for very different "firework displays."

CLOCKWORK ORANGE
PURNULULU NATIONAL PARK,
KIMBERLEY, AUSTRALIA

Nature has superimposed several layers of these orange and black streaks with such incredible regularity that the Purnululu Range in the northwest of Australia is nothing short of amazing.

It took twenty million years to shape the sandstone (*purnululu* in aboriginal language) into steep-sloped cones and beehives, rising 820 feet above sea level. The horizontal stripes are in fact alternating rust-colored silica and dark lichen made up of microorganisms that protect the rock from accelerated erosion. This maze of cliffs also hides gorges and natural pools, surrounded by palm trees that grow from cracks in the rock. Plant and animal life abounds in the wet season. You can also spot future "hives" in formation from the beach in the north. In a few hundred thousand years, they will be able to join their peers. The Purnululu, also called Bungle Bungle, Range has only been known to the general public for the past quarter of a century, and was brought to our attention by a film crew. The park is still protected and only easily accessible by air.

This is no mirage: a hundred lakes punctuate this desert of dunes, about ▮ the size of New Jersey, located on the border of China and Inner Mongolia.

Over more than 19,000 square miles, star-shaped dunes and lakes fed by the snows of faraway Tibetan peaks stretch out as far as the eye can see: welcome to the paradoxical Badain Jaran desert. Some lakes are filled with fresh water; others, with high rates of evaporation, are saturated with salt and bacteria that encourage the proliferation of red algae. These water holes are not fed by rain – no more than 1.5 inches a year – but by underground springs, themselves fed by the Tibetan glaciers of the Qilian Mountains, hundreds of miles away. Even if this desert is no longer the Eden it once was thousands of years ago, thirty Mongolian families still live there on the basis of "one lake, one family" separated by these stationary dunes. Bilitu (1,640 feet), nicknamed the Everest of the sands, is one of the highest dunes in the world. At nightfall, these sand mountains sing and sigh: the mystery of Badain Jaran remains intact.

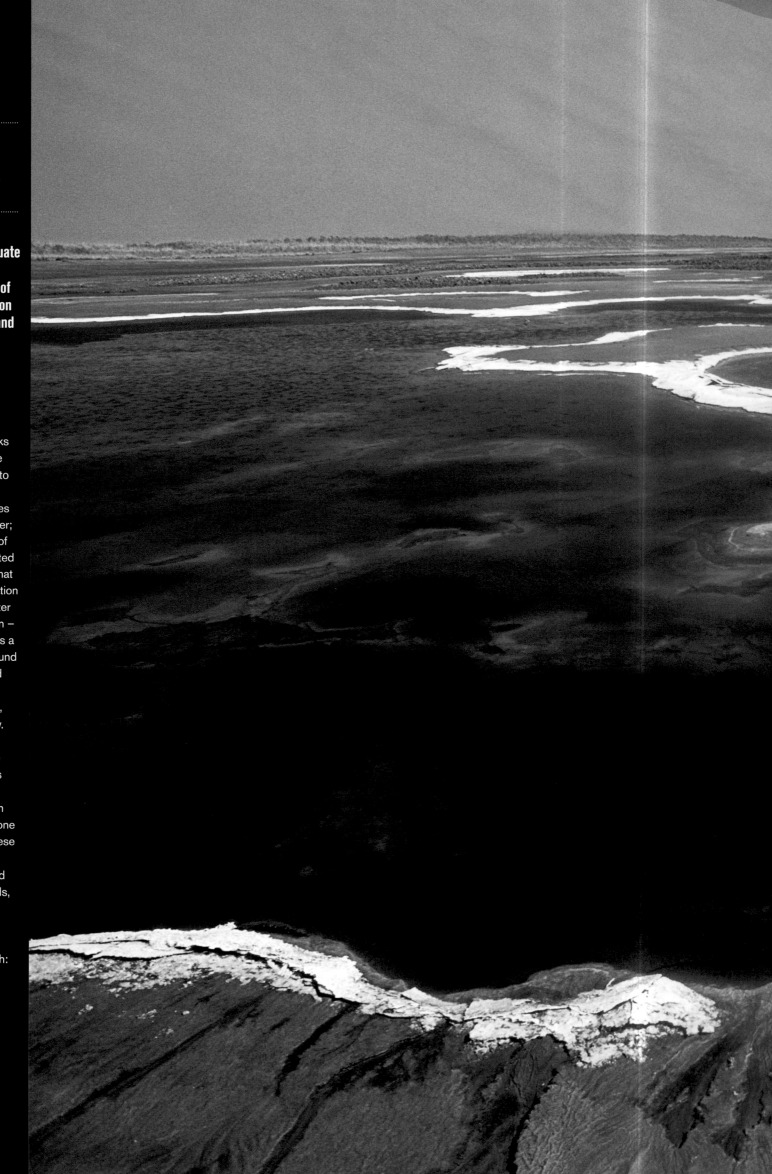

Four miles of pure white sandy beaches lined with the turquoise blue waters of the Coral Sea make for a dazzling paradise. Sunglasses are a must!

Whitehaven Bay is known as THE beach. It is indeed indisputably unique. A huge oasis of white sand located on one of the largest of the Whitsunday Islands, along the coral reef, it is a picture-perfect incarnation of paradise on Earth. The 74 Whitsunday Islands are the emerged parts of an old volcanic mountain range covered by the sea in the Ice Age. Geologists have determined that the white sands are not local, but rather result from a long drift of silica along the coasts of Queensland. Rid of its impurities and heavy mineral sands, all that is left is 99% pure white quartz, sand that is so fine, it could be used to make glass or polish jewelry. Faced with such a sight, we recommend heading for the heights and seeking shade under the large pine trees of Hill Inlet, which offers the best views of the twists and turns created by the currents, in shades ranging from white to blue.

CHALKBOARD
ETRETAT CLIFFS, NORMANDY, FRANCE

The Etretat cliffs have inspired many artists over the centuries, such as the author Guy de Maupassant, the painter Claude Monet and the writer of the Arsène Lupin detective novels, Maurice Leblanc.

Three "gates", the "needle", the "room for ladies" and the "manhole": the names for the distinctive formations of the Etretat cliffs evoke the majesty and mystery of the site, which is captured in paintings by Courbet, Boudin and Monet. The top of these white limestone cliffs is a sheer 300-foot drop to the Channel. The rain has sculpted this Pays de Caux coast over the centuries and the water seeping through the porous limestone has eroded the rock, leading to masses of fallen rocks. The limestone dissolved in the sea while layers of flint, polished by the waves, washed up as grey pebbles on the beach. The Amont, Aval and Manneporte gates were created by a coastal river, which channeled its way into the cliff before receding. Only the hardest limestone and granite parts of the rock resisted. The sea then progressively widened the arches and sharpened the hollow needle. Who knows, there might still be a few hidden treasures not yet discovered by the detective Arsène Lupin…

JURASSIC PARK
SAN RAFAEL SWELL, UTAH,
UNITED STATES

Utah was once a haven for dinosaurs, before they disappeared during the Ice Age. Researchers have found some 15,000 bones belonging to these extinct giants.

The San Rafael Swell, a giant sandstone, shale and limestone crease or wave running across Utah, came about when the Earth's crust shifted millions of years ago. This geological feature led to the erosion of hundreds of feet of sediment left by the sea, leaving a landscape that strangely resembles the planet Mars. These ground movements also brought to light an incredible treasure: one of the most important sites in the world for fossilized dinosaur bones. The preserved remains of 70 different animals, including 11 species – for the most part carnivores – were unearthed over the course of a century, ever since a stockbreeder came across a giant "sheep bone." How and why did these monsters that once ruled the Earth end up in this giant graveyard? Scientists are still battling with that one.

DOWNPOURS
STORM OVER ARIZONA,
UNITED STATES

From the famous oracles of Ancient Times, man has tried to forecast the weather, and more specifically meteorological disturbances, but has not yet reached an exact science.

Thunderstorms are one of the most spectacular weather phenomena, particularly when accompanied by electrical discharge (thunder and lighting) or torrential rain. In any case, this is an outward sign of the air's unsettled nature, with a contrast between high humidity and dryer air at higher altitudes. A trigger, such as great heat or a passing cold front, also needs to be part of the equation. It all starts with big or small storm clouds, some covering up to 300 miles. The exchange of air masses inside these cumuli transforms the condensed steam into ice crystals. The temperature can fall to -4°F at the cloud top. When the storm has fully developed, these crystals melt into large or small raindrops that can either evaporate before reaching the ground or, on the contrary, turn into pouring rain. When the worst of the storm has passed, the cloud top frays into the shape of an anvil, a sight we often miss hiding under our umbrellas…

CHOCOLATE AND WHIPPED CREAM
WILLIAM RIVER,
SASKATCHEWAN, CANADA

Seen from the sky, this sight can be described as mouth-watering: among the pistachio-green forests and white whipped cream dunes, a chocolate river flows out into one of the largest Canadian lakes.

The William River is a watercourse prone to mood swings. Fast paced and deep at its source, on its way it picks up tons of sand and sediment that slow down its progress over approximately twenty miles, before finally reaching Lake Athabasca. Its load makes for surrealist colors, all in shades of brown and caramel. In fact, the William River crosses amazing landscapes: on the one side, it runs along giant sand dunes more than 100 feet tall and half a mile long, and on the other, a forest of jack pines, birch and spruce, typical of the Saskatchewan region. To stop human mining activity from damaging this picture postcard, the dunes were turned into a natural park twenty years ago. Like back in the times of the fur trade, the canoe remains the best method of transportation to admire the show.

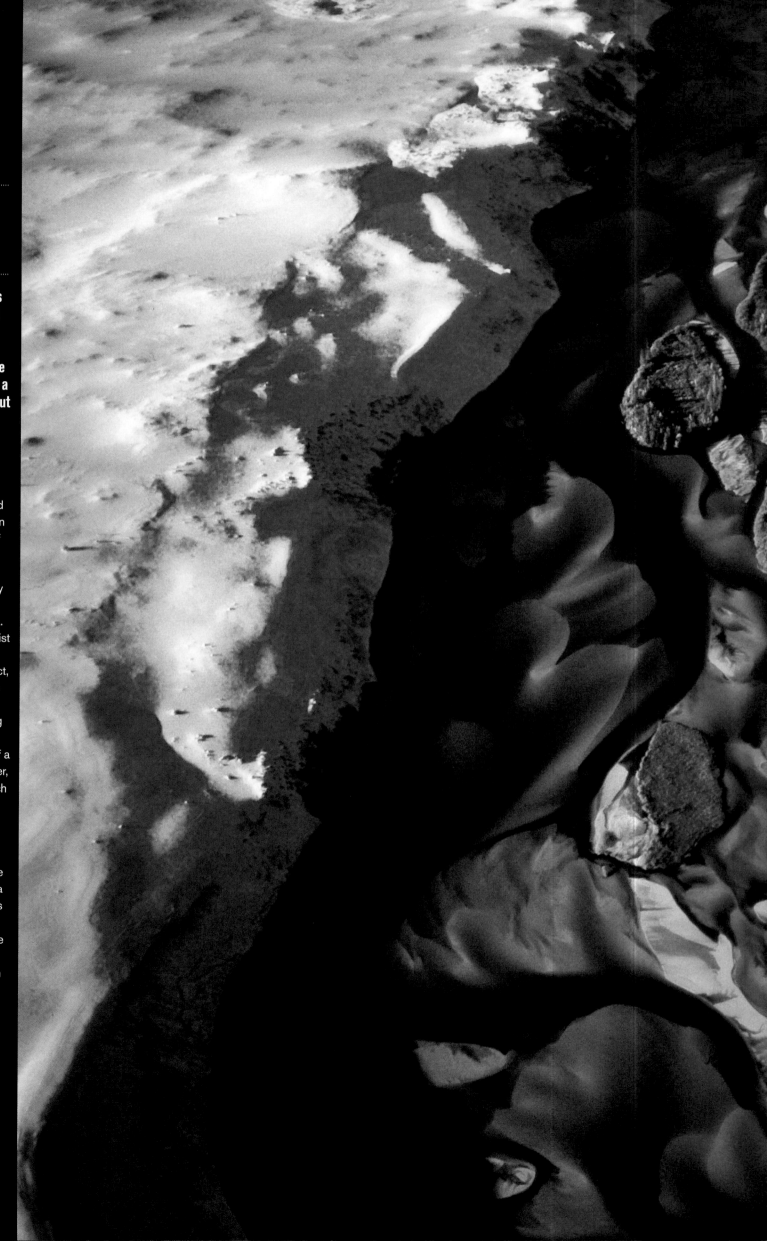

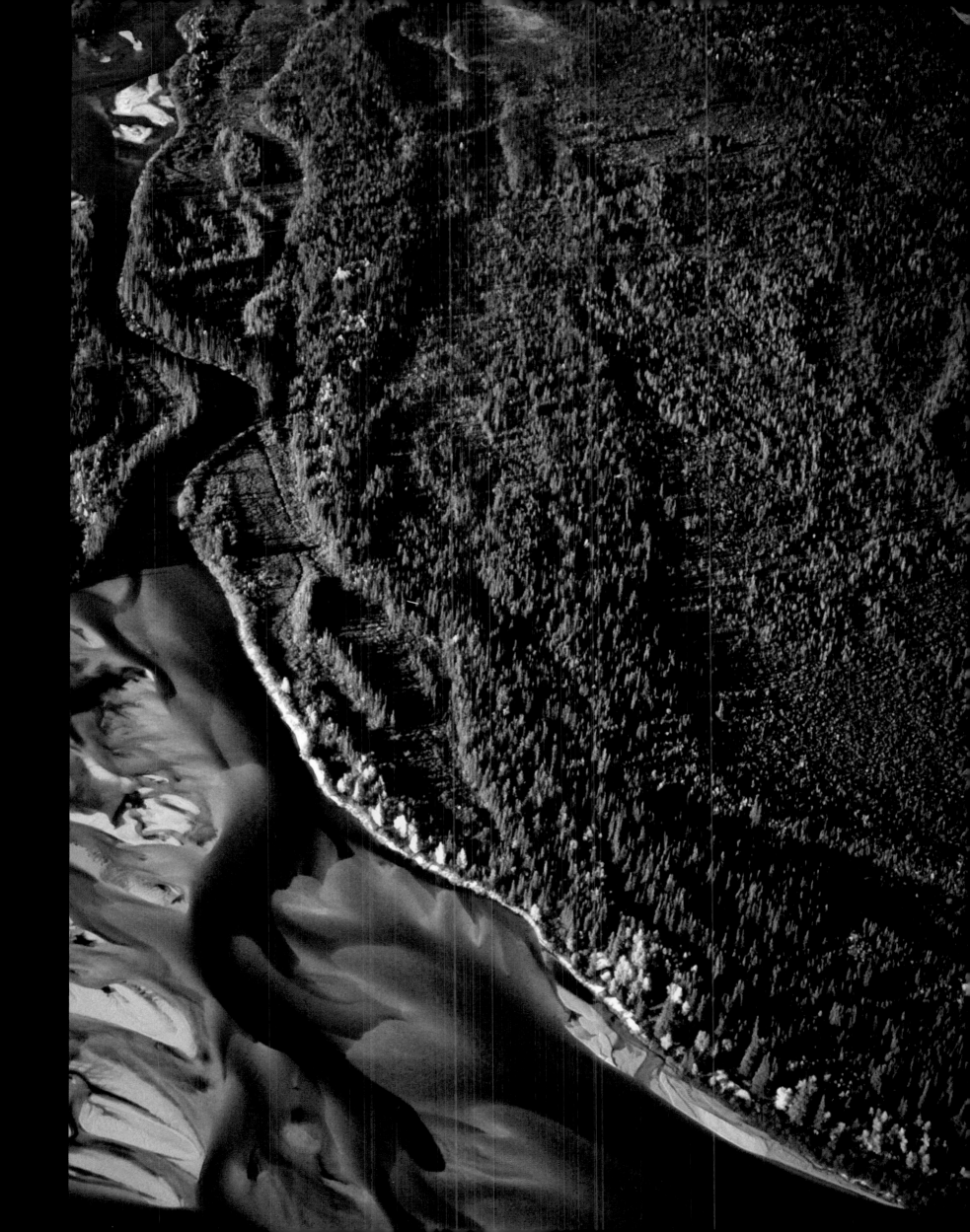

The Alps form a 745-mile long arc that crosses Europe from the Mediterranean Sea to the Danube, offering seven countries beautiful snowy slopes, from France to Austria.

Even if the highest Alpine peaks tend to be found more to the west (in France, for example, where the Mont Blanc rises 15,781 feet above sea level), Austria, a mountainous country if ever there was one, counts a few fine peaks of 11,500 to 12,500 feet, such as the Grossglockner or the Wildspitze in the Tyrol and Hohe Tauern mountain ranges. The name "Alps" appeared before the birth of Jesus Christ, in the days of Hannibal and his famous war elephants! Whether the word has Gallic or Eurasian origins, it describes high summits, dating back more than 200 million years, when the African and the European plates converged. Of the huge ice cap that once covered these mountainous regions, only 1,500 square miles remain, in Italy, Switzerland, France and Austria. In the spring, they flow into great rivers such as the Rhine, the Rhône and the Pô, not to mention the tributaries of the beautiful blue Danube.

FROM YESTERDAY TO TOMORROW
DIOMEDE ISLAND, ALASKA,
UNITED STATES

The International Date Line passes in between the American Little Diomede and its big Russian sister. A tunnel will one day perhaps link today and tomorrow.

When the mist finally decides to clear, the Diomede Islands seem to appear out of nowhere, in the middle of a sea of ice and bluish reflections. The two rocky islands, located right in the middle of the Bering Strait, are the remains of an ancient land bridge between the two continents. These tuyas, once flat-topped, steep-sloped volcanic mountains measuring 820 to 980 feet, are barren of vegetation. Fauna is also non-existent in these parts, except below the surface of the water. One hundred and fifty Inuit, gathered in a single village, live on Little Diomede, much in the same way as in the days of the first hunting camps. These islanders currently live in extreme conditions, but for how much longer? The project of digging a 60-mile tunnel passing through both isles is still being considered. Fifteen to twenty years of work would be needed if Russia and Alaska were to come to an agreement. But that won't happen overnight.

SEA GREEN
ZHUPANOV RIVER,
KRONOTSKY ZAPOVEDNIK
NATURE RESERVE, RUSSIA

In the land of hyperactive volcanoes, nature strives to adapt to the hostile conditions. Some remote areas were only discovered half a century ago but, man has already left his mark.

Nothing here is favorable: the weather, the strong winds that sweep over the nature reserve, the thick blanket of snow that covers everything for months on end, 85,000 acres of glacier, the constant threat of new volcanic eruptions… Despite all of this, the tundra, the grasslands and the forests have carved out a place for themselves among the swamps, lakes and rivers. Hydrothermal plants grow near hot water springs. In this frozen and volcanic vastness, you might be forgiven for thinking that man is insignificant. And yet… the wounds left by mining activity have not yet healed. The populations of brown bear, caribou and large grouse have been decimated, the forest of conifers cut down, and industrial fishing is putting certain marine mammals on a starvation diet. The danger does not only lie in the volcanoes.

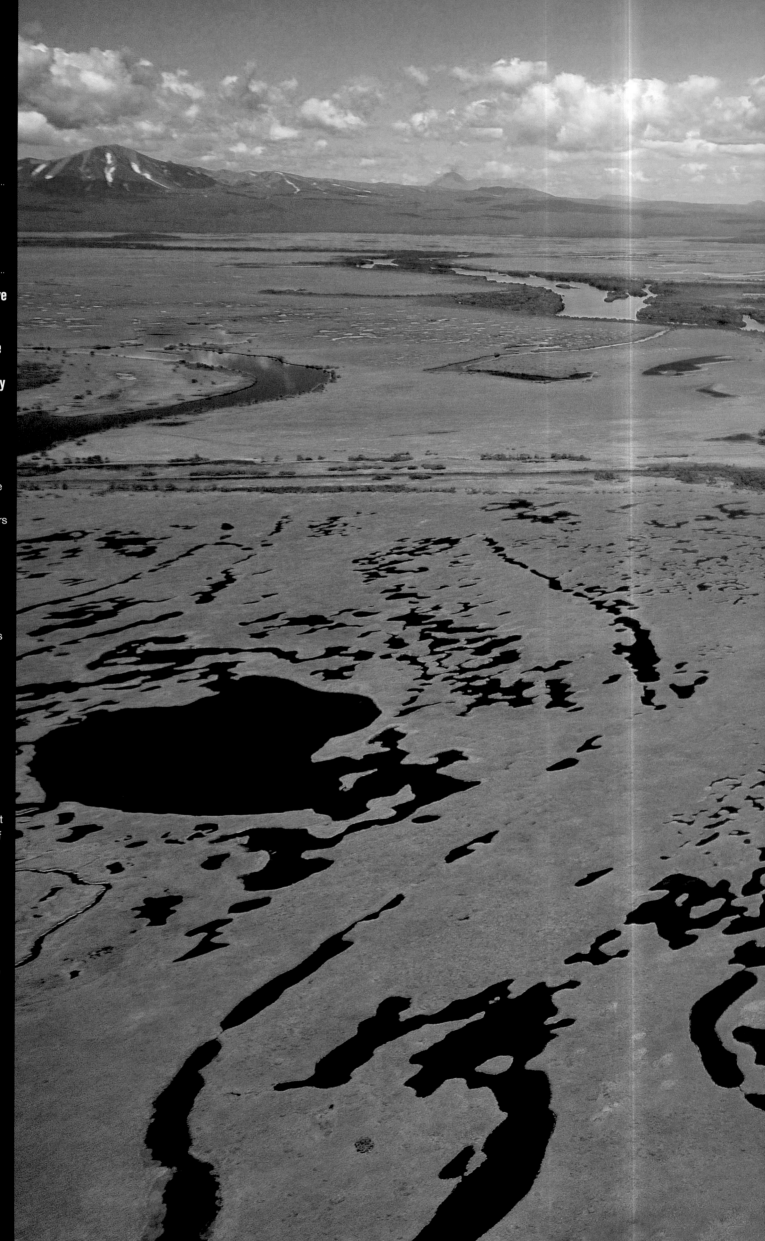

STONES AND EMERALDS
GORGES DU VERDON,
PROVENCE, FRANCE

Provence is very proud of this magnificent canyon– the tallest gorges in Europe – sometimes shrouded in mist and owing its name to the beautiful green color of its rivers and lakes.

The Verdon River winds its way amongst the 820- to 2,300-foot high limestone cliffs, measuring 20 to 330 feet wide at their base. Some of the most remarkable sites include the Styx du Verdon and the Imbut, a sort of funnel where the river disappears underground beneath a huge mass of rocks. These magnificent landscapes go back to the Jurassic period when a warm and shallow sea, carpeted with corals, covered the region of Provence. The birth of the Alps created faults in the limestone rocks, and the Verdon, once a turbulent river, channeled its way into the coral sediments. The sentry villages perched on the edge of the canyon are still as charming, whereas Salles sur Verdon has been built anew. The old market town was destroyed and submerged under the artificial lake of Sainte-Croix after the building of a dam in 1973.

This bay, said to be the most beautiful in the world, was once a place of refuge for pirates and the scene of naval battles. It now harbors hundreds of small fishing boats among its islands...

According to the legend of Ha Long (literally "Descending Dragon"), the dragon severed the mountain with his tail while in the throes of fighting the sea currents, leaving a string of some 2,000 sugarloaf islands and islets in the China Sea. These rocky peaks, scattered over 579 square miles, date back 250 to 280 million years, and were sculpted by erosion from the thick layer of sediment left by the sea. Rain and subterranean rivers have also hollowed out a number of caves, some leading to inner lakes and closing up again at high tide: an ideal hiding place, once for privateers, and now for hundreds of fishing families who live on the water… A little more than half of these islets are officially named. The "Dancing Dragon," the "Old Man Fishing," or the "Pair of Roosters" appear to sailors, like ghost ships, wreathed in the mysterious mist that always floats over Ha Long.

PICTURE CREDITS

The publisher would like to thank the following individuals and photographic libraires for permission to reproduce their material. Every care has been taken to trace copyright holders. However, if we have omitted anyone we apologize and will, if informed, make corrections to any future edition.

Pages 8-9 ©Doco Dalfiano/Photolibrary.com; 10-11 ©James P. Blair/Photolibrary. com; 12-13 ©Per-Andre Hoffmann/Photolibrary.com; 14-15 ©Moodboard RF/Photolibrary.com; 16-17 ©Norbert Wu/Science Faction/Corbis; 16-19 ©Kazuyoshi Nomachi/Corbis; 20-21 ©Lou Grive/Hoa-Qui/Eyedea; 22-23 ©Bob Krist/Corbis; 24-25 ©Image Source/Photolibrary.com; 26-27 ©Cameron Davidson/Getty; 28-29 ©Corbis/Photolibrary.com; 30-31 ©Jim Reed/Corbis; 32-33 ©Jonathan Blair/Corbis; 34-35 ©Tom Bean/Corbis; 36-37 ©Panorama Media/Photolibrary.com; 38-39 ©Chris Harris/Firstlight/Eyedea; 40-41 ©Cosmo Condina/Photolibrary.com; 42-43 ©Frans Lanting/Corbis; 44-45 ©Jim Richardson/Getty; 46-47 ©Enrique Aguirre/Photolibrary. com; 48-49 ©George Steinmetz/Corbis; 50-51 ©Eastcott Momatiuk/Getty; 52-53 ©Georg Gerster/Rapho/Eyedea; 54-55 ©Mond'Image./Photolibrary.com; 56-57 ©Chad Ehlers/Photolibrary.com; 58-59 ©J.A. Kraulis/Getty; 60-61 ©Frans Lanting/Corbis; 62-63 ©Egmont Strigl/Photolibrary.com; 64-65 ©Sampers E./Explorer/Hoa-Qui/Eyedea; 66-67 ©Franck Guiziou/Hemis/Corbis; 68-69 ©Frans Lanting/Corbis; 70-71 ©The Irish Image Collection/Photolibrary.com; 72-73 ©Michele Falzone/JAI/Corbis; 74-75 ©Jupiterimages/Getty; 76-77 ©Jim Richardson/Getty; 78-79 ©Ernst Wrba/Photolibrary. com; 80-81 ©David Clapp/Photolibrary.com; 82-83 ©Frank Krahmer/Getty; 84-85 ©Charles O'Rear/Corbis; 86-87 ©Photo 24/Photolibrary.com; 88-89 ©Theo Allofs/Corbis; 90-91 ©Danny Lehman/Corbis; 92-93 ©George Steinmetz/Corbis; 94-95 ©Jeff Foott/Getty; 96-97 ©Stephen Alvarez/Getty; 98-99 ©Kazuyoshi Nomachi/Corbis; 100-101 ©Bobby Haas/Getty; 102-103 ©Maria Stenzel/Getty; 104-105 ©Ricardo De Mattos/Getty; 106-107 ©Charles O'Rear/Corbis; 108-109 ©Serge Pottier; 110-111 ©Sakis Papadopoulos/Getty; 112-113 ©Yann Arthus-Bertrand/Corbis; 114-115 ©Brian Lawrence/Getty; 116-117 ©Frans Lanting/Corbis; 118-119 ©Michael T. Sedam/Corbis; 120-121 ©David Noton/Eyedea; 122-123 ©Philippe Bourseiller/Getty; 124-125 ©Photolibrary.com; 126-127 ©Frans Lanting/Corbis; 128-129 ©Frans Lanting/Corbis; 130-131 ©Corbis/Photolibrary. com; 132-133 ©Corbis/Photolibrary.com; 134-135 ©Jean Brooks/Getty; 136-137 ©Jim Reed Photography-Severe&/Corbis; 138-139 ©Arctic-Images/Getty; 140-141 Thorsten Milse/Photolibrary.com; 142-143 ©Fu Chunrong/Xinhua Press/Corbis; 144-145 ©Karlheinz Irlmeier/Photolibrary.com; 146-147 ©Bourseillier Philippe/Hoa-Qui/Eyedea; 148-149 ©Shah Anup/Jacana/Eyedea; 150-151 ©152/Photolibrary. com; 152-153 ©Morand-Grahame Gérald/Hoa-Qui/Eyedea; 154-155 ©Paul Lawrence/Photolibrary.com; 156-157 ©Hans Stranc/Corbis; 158-159 ©Keren Su/ Corbis; 160-161 ©Imagemore Co, Ltd./Getty; 162-163 ©Chad Ehlers/Photolibrary. com; 164-165 ©Gerd Ludwig/Corbis; 166-167 ©Robert Francis/Photolibrary.com; 168-169 ©Alberto Garcia/Corbis; 170-171 ©Theo Allofs/Corbis; 172-173 ©Bobby Haas/Getty; 174-175 ©JTB Photo/Photolibrary.com; 176-177 ©Olivier Grunewald/ Photolibrary.com; 178-179 ©Bobby Haas/Getty; 180-181 ©Philippe Bourseiller/ Getty; 182-183 ©Barcroft Media via Getty Images; 184-185 ©Ludo Kuipers/Corbis; 186-187 ©George Steinmetz/Corbis; 188-189 ©George Steinmetz/Corbis; 190-191 ©DELU Ch./Hoa-Qui/Eyedea; 192-193 ©Frans Lanting/Corbis; 194-195 ©Georg Gerster/Rapho/Eyedea; 196-197 ©Craig Aurness/Corbis; 198-199 ©Neil Emmerson/Corbis; 200-201 ©National Geographic/Getty Images/Getty; 202-203 ©Igor Shpilenok/NPL/Jacana/Eyedea; 204-205 ©age fotostock/Photolibrary.com; 206-207 ©Rene Mattes/Photolibrary.com.